A MEMOIR

THE ELEPHANT GATES

Vibrant Reflections of Life, Family, and Tradition in Sri Lanka

Chamalee Namal Weeratunge

Published by River Grove Books
Austin, TX
www.rivergrovebooks.com

Distributed by River Grove Books

For ordering information or special discounts for bulk purchases, please contact River Grove Books at PO Box 91869, Austin, TX 78709, 512.891.6100.

Design and composition by Greenleaf Book Group
Cover design by Greenleaf Book Group

Cataloging-in-Publication data
Weeratunge, Chamalee Namal.
The elephant gates : vibrant reflections of life, family, and tradition in Sri Lanka : a memoir / Chamalee Namal Weeratunge.—First edition.
pages : illustration, map ; cm
Issued also as an ebook.
1. Weeratunge, Chamalee Namal. 2. Depānama (Sri Lanka)—Social life and customs—20th century. 3. Sri Lanka—Biography. 4. Autobiography. I. Title.
DS489.83 .W44 2014
954.93032092 2014943724

Print ISBN: 978-1-63299-001-3
eBook ISBN: 978-1-63299-002-0

First Edition

For Thāththi.

The author as a child at the Elephant Gates, 1971

Contents

Acknowledgments

Nalini Weerasinghe; for her steadfast willingness to lend me her time and attention in reviewing the material for this book.

Jayati Weerakoon; for the thoughtful insights and helpful suggestions he provided me with after reviewing my work.

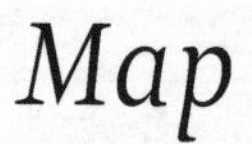

DEPĀNAMA
AND
SURROUNDING
AREA

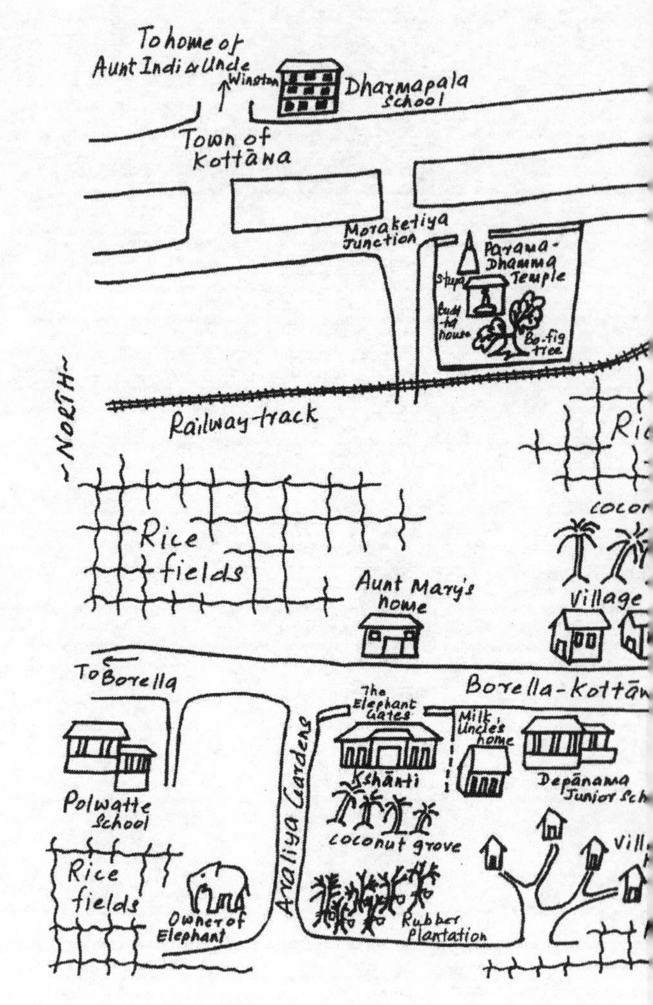

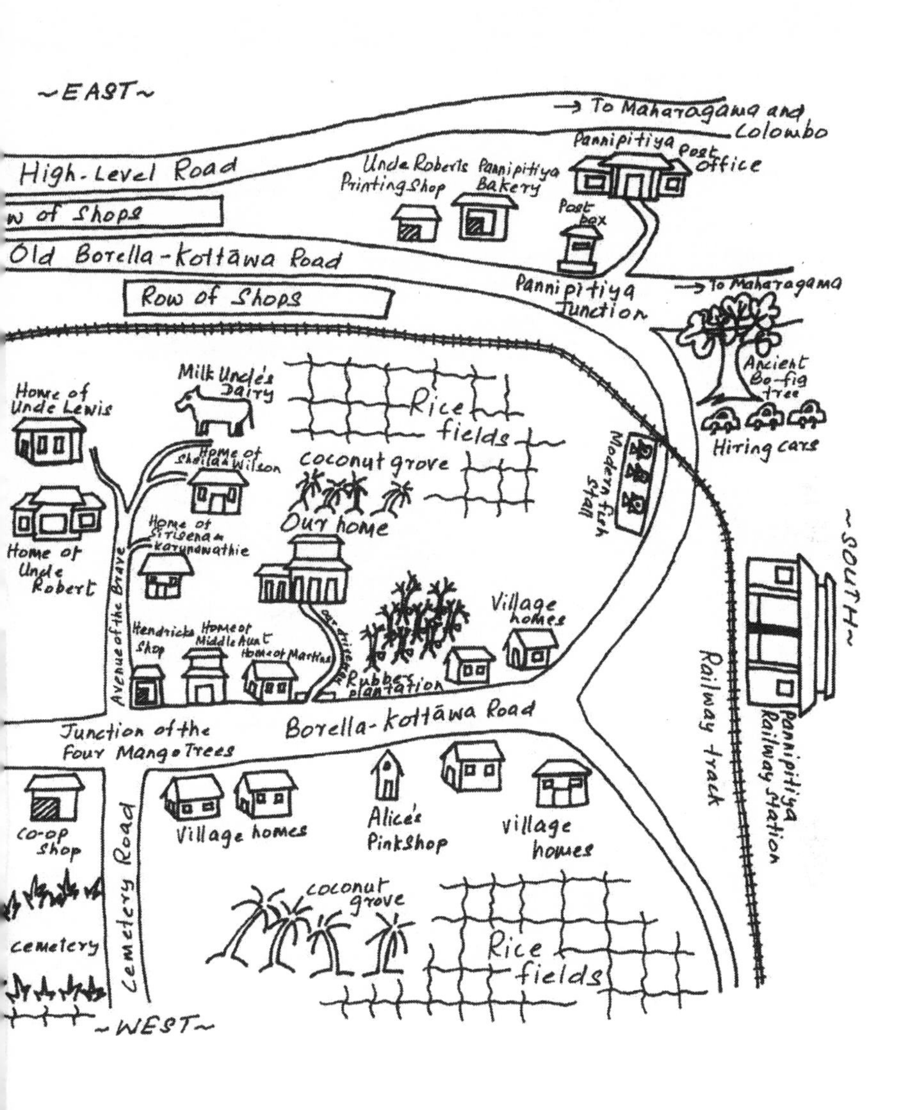
~EAST~
→ To Maharagama and Colombo
High-Level Road
w of Shops
Uncle Roberts Printing Shop
Pannipitiya Bakery
Pannipitiya Post office
Post box
Old Borella-Kottāwa Road
Row of Shops
Pannipitiya Junction
→ To Maharagama
Ancient Bo-fig tree
Hiring cars
Milk Uncle's Dairy
Rice fields
Home of Uncle Lewis
Home of Sheila Wilson
coconut grove
Modern fish Stall
Home of Uncle Robert
Home of Sirisena & Karunawathie
Our home
~SOUTH~
Village homes
Hendricks Shop
Home of Middle Aunt
Home of Martha
Rubber plantation
Avenue of the Brave
Railway track
Pannipitiya Railway Station
Junction of the Four Mango Trees
Borella-kottāwa Road
Co-op Shop
Village homes
Alice's Pink Shop
village homes
Cemetery Road
coconut grove
cemetery
Rice fields
~WEST~

Introduction

The Elephant Gates is a collection of narratives that have endured the passage of time from childhood to adulthood. They have travelled with me from the continent of my birth to the one I have eventually settled in. It is a whimsical look back at growing up in the village of Depānama on the island of Sri Lanka, in the 1970s up to the mid-1980s, three decades or so following several centuries of European colonial occupation. During my childhood spent in the village, the last of these colonial vestiges were being shed, and an era of industrialization and mechanization was slowly dawning. Some of the terminology and phrasing used in this book reflect this colonial influence and some others reflect the changing times.

Central to each essay is Āchchā, my maternal grandmother, and Kshānti, the home she lived in, the ancestral home of my mother in Depānama. Today, Depānama is yet another suburb of the capital of Colombo, indistinguishable from most others. In this collection, I have vividly described what must have been everyday and mundane occurrences at the time, to bring to life people who are now gone, places that are now changed, and customs that have now become redundant.

The story of how Depānama got its name has been lost within its centuries-old history, but the two syllables making up the word *Depānama* mean "At your feet I pay homage." To do justice to its name, my collection pays homage to my cherished village and its memorable inhabitants. Some of those most dear to me, including Āchchā herself and my father, have passed away. My aunts and uncles are now grandparents, and all my cousins, who were as close to me as if they were my own siblings, have migrated to different parts of the world and are raising families of their own.

My family was affected by pain, loss, scandal, and despair, just as much as any other family in the village. Social injustice, inequality, and intolerance were part of the fabric of life in my village, just as much as in any other. These narratives are not an historical record, but rather a child's perspective of how things were. My memories have left me with an aching nostalgia for a simpler time and place. These are stories of that time and place.

I

The House with the Elephant Gates

Depānama has not had the distinction of having centuries of its history meticulously chronicled, as have the distinguished cities in the North and in the South. It has not received any honorable mention in the ancient scripts as a center of religion, art, or commerce. There has been no ancient monarch, however long or short his reign, who has called it his home. There are no pillars of granite, statues of stone, or other priceless artifacts to be excavated.

The hamlet which became known as Depānama lies about twelve miles to the south of the capital city of Colombo. People who were said to have originally hailed from the South settled it. No evidence other than hearsay exists today for or against this hypothesis. If such a migration did occur, it must have occurred several hundred years prior to my birth in the village of Depānama.

The first settlers must have arrived by bullock cart in search of land for the cultivation of rice. The marshes must have been discovered and plowed. The lattice of rice beds must have been flooded to just the right depth, and the first rice seeds sown. News of this rich harvest must have caused more to come. Rubber must have grown wherever rice could not.

Where neither rice nor rubber could be grown, coconut and spices must have flourished. The ancestors of my maternal grandfather must have been amongst the first to arrive.

Depānama had always been fortunate in that there had never been destructive floods or prolonged periods of drought. Never had there been a recorded hurricane, nor mudslide, nor epidemic, nor famine. The earth beneath this serene place was not violated by a fault, and thus no earthquake would ever shake its serenity. The crop-sustaining monsoon never failed in its arrival twice a year.

The main road that ran across Depānama was named the Borella-Kottāwa Road. When first constructed, it must have been a narrow dirt road, though eventually it was broadened and tarred. The Borella-Kottāwa Road linked the town of Kottāwa on the one end to the town of Borella on the other. Many villages lay along this major thoroughfare, like pearls on a necklace, of which Depānama was but one precious pearl.

Both Borella and Kottāwa were larger towns and must have been settled much earlier than Depānama. Both Borella and Kottāwa lay along direct trade routes to the capital of Colombo. Whatever trade took place in Depānama took place alongside the Borella-Kottāwa Road. Property along this road was of prime value. My relatives on my mother's side, having found Depānama to be a suitable locality to inhabit many centuries ago, settled alongside the Borella-Kottāwa Road.

In the early days, every family in Depānama was descended from one of three families, of which my grandfather's family was one. These families owned many hectares of land on both sides of the Borella-Kottāwa Road, down to the rice fields in one direction and the rubber plantations in the other. They also owned the rice fields and the rubber plantations. New families must have arrived with time and established their own lineage. To some of them land was sold, and to others land was gifted in recognition of service or as means of payment for services rendered. This was the custom in those days when land was plentiful. Schools, temples, and public offices were built on land gifted by these landowning families, though with time these altruistic acts were forgotten. At the time of marriage, land was given away to children as dowries. Large acreages were split among siblings when the land passed from parents to their offspring. Often neighbors were siblings, and neighboring properties could trace their origins back to many generations of ancestors within the same family.

The property on which Kshānti, the ancestral home of my mother, was built stood facing the Borella-Kottāwa Road in the center of Depānama. It had belonged to the family of my grandfather for several generations, and for generations ancestral homes had been built, renovated, demolished, and rebuilt upon its soil. Upon the death of his parents, the property was portioned into two, my grandfather inheriting one half and his younger brother the other. The rice fields, rubber plantations, and other lands were also bequeathed and eventually passed on to one or another of his five siblings.

After his marriage to Āchchā, my grandmother, and while his daughters were still young, my grandfather demolished the old house as his predecessors had done. He built his own home to fit his specifications and the needs of his family. When its construction was complete, he invited the monk Sumanatissa from the Temple of Parama-Dhamma to give it a name. The name that was chosen, "Kshānti," traces its origin to the ancient language of Sanskrit. It meant "patience" or "forbearance." At the time of the renovation, in accordance with the architectural style of the day, a wall was constructed to shield and separate the house and grounds from the roadside. The entrance was adorned with a pair of wrought iron gates that met in the middle when closed. Each half was hung with iron hinges and secured into the masonry of two cement pillars that faced each other. A figure of an elephant with trunk raised, symbolizing homage and hospitality, was fashioned into the iron works of each half of the gate. When the Elephant Gates at Kshānti closed, the elephant of one half of the gate met the other with trunk raised.

Kshānti was constructed along the design dictates followed by many of the larger homes in the village. The veranda ran along the front of the house and faced the road. There were two rooms, one to the left and one to the right of the veranda. The one to the left was the office room used by my grandfather. Six sets of folding glass doors separated the veranda from the main living room of the house. The living room was flanked on either side by four additional rooms. A hallway led from the back of the living room to a large dining room on the right. The kitchen led off the very end of the hallway. A bathroom was later added opposite the dining room, but when the house was first built, the bathroom was not a part of the main house; instead there was an outhouse at the back of the garden.

Fruit trees were planted around the house for shade. A grove of coconut palms and spicebushes were planted in the back to supply the household with these essential ingredients and condiments.

Depānama was not fitted with power lines and towers to receive the hydro-electricity produced by the cascading falls originating in the hill country. Its homes, however large or small, were without electricity when Kshānti was first built. As children, my mother and aunts did their homework and ate their dinner by lamplight. There was not the luxury of running water in the house either. All water used in the house was drawn manually from a well at least fifty feet deep at the bottom of the property and brought to the house in buckets. By the time I was born, more modern amenities had become established in Depānama and I was glad of that.

As a young man my grandfather left home to apprentice with a physician specializing in traditional Ayurvedic medicine. He did so when his mother, my great-grandmother, was stricken with blindness. He returned home with a specialized knowledge in the diseases of the eye and cures for eye ailments. He did not find a cure for what ailed his mother, but he did become widely known for his treatment of eye disorders. His gift for healing was not surprising as many of his cousins were well known locally, and even beyond, for the practice of Ayurvedic medicine. In the back garden at Kshānti, massive cauldrons simmered over slow wood fires for days, brewing mixtures, potions, and elixirs condensed from roots, barks, and leaves for his healing potions and salves. This was not an age when the art of healing was practiced for profit by the healer. Healing was a gift, practiced with the aim of restoring the health and well-being of the afflicted. It was a way of life for the gifted, but not a means of livelihood. Gratitude and thanks were expressed in words alone. A sheaf of beetle leaves was sometimes presented to the healer as a mark of appreciation and show of reverence, but nothing more.

With the passage of time and recognition of his service to the village, my grandfather was appointed headman of the village of Depānama. This was a position that had been held by his father and his father's father, but was by no means an inherited station or status. His duties as headman transformed the house of Kshānti into the political center of the village. From here laws were enforced, disputes were mediated, and squabbles were settled.

Araliya Gardens, a small dirt road, ran along the right side of the property of Kshānti, through sparse scrub jungle and rubber plantations that eventually led to the rice fields. To the left of Kshānti was the property of the Milk Uncle, the younger brother of my grandfather. Beyond this was the Depānama Junior School where the children of Depānama attended from grades one to five. Those who graduated from the Junior School were promoted to The Dharmapala School near Kottāwa. My mother and aunts had all graduated from The Dharmapala School. My parents had met there when still teenagers.

The house directly across the road from Kshānti had a matriarch of its own—a crony and contemporary of Āchchā named Mary. My mother and aunts called her "Aunt Mary," not in recognition of a blood relationship but in recognition of the close friendship that she and Āchchā shared. She accompanied Āchchā to the temple when Āchchā needed company and often dropped by for a chat and cup of tea in the afternoons. We did not know of the early history of Aunt Mary in the village but my aunts did not openly talk about it. They chose to leave her past buried in her past. Aunt Mary lived with her son, daughter-in-law, their children, and her unmarried daughter. She was one of only a few trusted confidants that Āchchā kept company with after her retirement.

After the death of her husband, Āchchā did not find herself alone. She was mother to four daughters and soon found herself mother-in-law to four sons-in-law and grandmother to eight grandchildren, five of them girls and three of them boys. They gave her plenty of things to do. The life that she had shared with her husband, in Depānama, in their home Kshānti, had come to an end, at least in this life. She did not involve herself in village affairs as she had done when her husband was alive. She was content instead to observe its goings-on through the Elephant Gates.

2

Grace

Āchchā, my maternal grandmother, had been named Grace at birth. It seemed a most unlikely name for Āchchā, who both in appearance and character was more robust than graceful. In giving her this name her mother may have envisioned Āchchā in her own image, as a demure woman of petite stature. It is said of Āchchā's mother, my great-grandmother, that she rarely ventured out of her home. She was a lady from the town of Panadura. Her upbringing is said to have been sheltered and religious.

When my great-grandmother married, she moved to the town of Gangodawila, the home of my great-grandfather. About ten miles separated the two towns, but this was a great distance in those days, when most travelled by bullock-drawn cart. The marriage was an arrangement between the two families. The wedding was a grand affair. The groom and his relatives escorted brides of the time to their new homes in a procession many bullock carts long. My great-grandmother's relatives would have traveled with her to continue on with the festivities for several more days. Her parents must have sent with her such luxuries as bedding, curtaining, and table linens of soft cotton. Cart after cart overflowing with fruits, vegetables, grains, cereals, spices, utensils, and furniture would have brought up the rear of the cart train, leaving no doubt among onlookers that the prosperity of the bride was abundant and excessive. Once the journey was made, though, one rarely travelled back, even for visits.

Āchchā sometimes spoke to me of her mother, as did my aunts of their grandmother. She was a woman of very fair complexion, they said. She lightened her complexion further by the application of perfumed talcum powder to her face, as was the custom then. Having been born and raised during the colonial occupation, she dressed very much in the Victorian style, in floor-length skirts and high-necked long-sleeved blouses of fine lace. Her disposition is said to have been childlike. In fact, when her first child was born lifeless, my great-grandfather is said to have brought home a doll to console her. But then, in defiance of her delicate disposition, she bore eleven more children, and thus, Āchchā was blessed with ten siblings. I had known only three of Āchchā's siblings and they were all petite. The youngest of her sisters, Padma, had lived with her own family in the ancestral home at Gangodawila, as was required by the youngest child to do. The black sheep of her siblings was a younger brother who ran away from home at an early age and became a vagabond. No news of his exploits had been received in years, and so it was misinformation, rather than information, that created a legend of dark tales and fantasy around this brother who was known in the family as the "Thieving Brother."

Āchchā was tall, broadly built, and dark in complexion. She took after her father, in appearance at least. She was slow and unhurried in her movements. She consumed her meals at the large dining table in the dining room at the back of the house. She took her midmorning and afternoon teas in the armchair on the veranda looking out over the Borella-Kottāwa Road. She listened to sermons on the little red pocket radio my father brought her from one of his trips abroad. When she left the house on an errand, she did so on foot. For these short walks she wore a sari in the Indian style and leather slippers. She clutched her purse under her arm and held her umbrella in her hand.

Āchchā's umbrella was one of her most treasured possessions. She never left the house without it. When she opened it up and held it over her head, it sheltered her from the sun and the rain. When she held it directly in front of her, it became a shield against the wind and stopped her sari from blowing out around her. When folded up, it became a stick in case of attack by an unfriendly dog or poisonous snake. She hoped that the umbrella in her hand would deter a jewelry snatcher from snatching her gold necklace and bangles. It may be this, but Āchchā had never had her necklace or bangles snatched. Āchchā's personal possessions were few and she placed a high value on items of versatility and utility. For beauty alone she had no use. If she valued her gold jewelry, it was only because she intended to leave it to her children.

If Āchchā was robust in appearance and action, she was even more so in character. I had never known Āchchā to cry out in pain when she was hurt. She seldom complained about her health when she felt unwell. She was not given to fits of emotion, giggles, or rowdy laughter. She never raised her voice in anger or frustration. She talked only about things that needed to be talked about, and rarely about things that did not. When she gossiped, she did so matter-of-factly.

It may have been will or it may have been circumstance that prompted Āchchā to choose a career. She trained and started work as a teacher. First, at the large girls' school in Maharagama and, later, at the smaller village school in Polwatte about half a mile down the Borella-Kottāwa Road from Depānama.

At the age of thirty-six, an age when for many at that time a life of spinsterhood was all but a certainty, Āchchā married. Our village was not the village Āchchā was born in. Our village was the village of Depānama, another ten miles or so southeast of Gangodawila. She moved to Depānama upon her marriage to my grandfather, her first and only love. But if Āchchā ever felt like a stranger within the confines of the village, she never gave any indication of it. It was as if she had always belonged to the village and the village to her.

She never spoke to me of how she arrived in Depānama as a new bride. I doubt that a lavish bullock cart wedding procession was commissioned, as in the case of her mother. It may have been that my grandfather hired a car and driver at the junction of Pannipitiya and escorted her to his home.

Āchchā bore four children—none of them a son. If she was unhappy at the prospect of lacking an heir to carry the name of her husband, she did not show it. If the prospect of securing a suitable husband for each of her daughters had ever burdened her, she must have borne it well. She was not only robust, but also proud.

She may have found her firstborn, my mother, to be stubborn, given to exerting her opinions with an unforgiving will. She may have found her second child, my Aunt Indi, most likely her favorite, to be happy, carefree, and easily given to whimsy. Her third, my Middle Aunt, had manifested a tendency to challenge authority even as a child, and when she married my Uncle Devapiya of her own choosing, rejecting the marriage that Āchchā had chosen for her, it was as if she had fulfilled a prophesy. Her last born, my Youngest Aunt, was truly the baby of the family—patient, impressionable, and willing to follow the dictates of tradition. If Āchchā was sometimes exasperated at these traits in her children, she did not show her disappointment. She spoke of them only with fondness.

Āchchā's arrival in Depānama also heralded the launch of her political life as the spouse of the village headman, a position my grandfather bore. At the time her first daughter was born, independence from colonial rule was within sight, only but a few years away. The prospect of the eventual establishment of a self-governing democracy ignited a palpable excitement within the national conscience and a new political awareness emerged in the village. Two parties, the party of the Hand and the party of the Elephant, vied for power even before liberation occurred. The village was firmly divided, Hand vs. Elephant. The Elephant was liberal, its policies more in line with those of the West. The Hand was more conservative, its leaders spearheading a nationalistic movement to take the nation back to a precolonial era. My grandfather had served the village as its headman under colonial rule, a position he was assured even after such rule ended. It was only expected that he should back the Elephant. The campaigning, Āchchā said, was energetic. Pamphlets were printed and distributed, meetings and parades were held. Mud and cow dung were freely slung at the houses of the Hand supporters in the dead of night. Once party lines were drawn and loyalties declared, families in the village feuded for generations to follow.

Āchchā often remarked upon how tumultuous those times were. Regardless of how dirty the village politics got, its domestic squabbles needed to be resolved fairly and squarely without the prejudice of party leanings. My grandfather's office, from where he conducted his duties, lay immediately to the left of the veranda, and could be accessed without traversing the house. If the disputes brought to his door became violent and loud, the main part of the house could be closed off for safety. Āchchā was her husband's closest and most trusted comrade. Political camaraderie had always been a part of their relationship and of her relationship with the village. Āchchā was considered one of the foremost authorities on all things in the village.

None of Āchchā's eight grandchildren had met her husband, our grandfather, for we were all born after his death. She described him to us as tall, slim, and fair in complexion. "I was the dark one, and he, the fair one," she joked. His attire was in keeping with the office he held. He wore a long sarong, as did most men of the day. Tucked neatly into the sarong, he wore a crisp white shirt. A leather belt and buttoned long-sleeved jacket completed the ensemble. His long hair was held back at the nape of his neck in a little bun the size of an *arecanut*—the seed of the tall and slender Areca palm, a little larger than a nutmeg seed. His hair was further secured with a rounded tortoiseshell comb. A full-length photograph of him hung in Āchchā's room. When she spoke of him, even as a child I could sense her yearning for him.

When I, the eldest of her grandchildren, was born, Āchchā had retired as a teacher and sometimes-politician. She was now content to observe the village from within the Elephant Gates, from the comfort of the armchair in the open veranda at Kshānti. This was her favorite spot. The bright sunlight outside threw a dark shadow over the veranda. Āchchā, in her favorite spot, was virtually unnoticed by passersby along the Borella-Kottāwa road. Every now and then an old acquaintance would stop at the Elephant Gates and squint to spot her, hoping to be invited in for a chat and cup of tea.

The arrangement of the marriage of my Youngest Aunt, Āchchā's fourth daughter, to a young man from the distant town of Puwakpitiya saw the last of her duties done. My Youngest Aunt and her husband, now my Uncle Dhaham, made their home in the ancestral house at Depānama, as was required by the youngest child to do upon marriage.

Āchchā relinquished the responsibility of the running of the house to the new couple. The third bedroom on the right side of the house held a table for her books, an *almirah*—a tall wooden cupboard with several compartments and drawers for her clothes—and a bed. This was all that was now hers.

3

The Rice Harvest

A SIMPLE SYSTEM OF ECONOMICS SEEMS to have existed in Depānama from the time it was first settled. Its wealth was the wealth of the rice fields. The wealthy owned the fields. Those who were not, worked on them. It was inevitable that rice should be a favored crop. Depānama possessed a broad network of low-lying tracks that trapped the rainwater from the two unfailing monsoons. It was this rain that coaxed the grains to germinate and shoot their tender sprouts through the mud. The scorching sun of the equally unfailing dry season that followed each monsoon teased out the golden grain until their heads bent over with weight and begged for the relief of the harvest.

I would not have expected any demanding species of rice that needed special care to have thrived in our fields, and they didn't. Instead, the strain that grew well and was thus chosen season after season was a large robust grain with a thick red-brown coating naturally resistant to pests, and able to survive most droughts and winds. Parboiling was the best way to tenderize it and yet preserve the nutrients in its coating. The rice flour it produced was red in color and tasted rough and fibrous. "Full of flavor," Āchchā used to say.

So it was that at the beginning of the sowing season when Āchchā, my father, and my Uncle Dhaham discussed the strain of rice to be sown, a sensible choice was made. Even though my grandfather's family had owned a fair acreage in rice fields when Depānama was first settled, subsequent marriages and disputes had led to their division. Of what remained, Āchchā, though retaining ownership, had relinquished charge of the harvest to my father and my Uncle Dhaham.

As a city dweller from the town of Maharagama, my father was unaccustomed to rice cultivation. Being a part-time rice farmer was a rite of passage to becoming a true villager. My father reveled in this role from the time he married my mother and moved to Depānama. If there was an enthusiasm that my father applied to his job as a marine engineer, oftentimes coming home from work stained with grease and smelling of the boiler room, he applied the same energy to farming. "He is like a child playing in the mud," my mother would observe, but as children we saw nothing wrong with playing in mud.

To my Uncle Dhaham, whose own ancestral home in Puwakpitiya overlooked many acres of rice, its cultivation came naturally. Oftentimes late in the night, Āchchā and her sons-in-law sat in the darkened veranda at Kshānti discussing in hushed voices the state of the crop and future decisions to be made.

My mother looked upon the cultivation of local rice with disfavor. She preferred that my father, by virtue of his important job in the city of Colombo and marriage to the eldest daughter of the former village headman, maintain a distance from the village farmers. She feared that if he did not clean his feet properly after a trip to the fields, he would catch a dangerous foot fungus. But more than her fears for his health, my mother feared that my father might breach decorum and partake of some coconut toddy offered to him by a villager.

If my Youngest Aunt felt the same way as my mother, she was not as insistent as my mother. My Uncle Dhaham was just as educated and just as importantly employed in Colombo, but in his case, as the son-in-law in charge of the ancestral home, maintaining old lands was an expected custom.

Rice was cultivated in two seasons coinciding with the arrival of the two monsoons, the *yala* in the first half of the year and the *maha* in the second half of the year. The fields themselves were divided into a pattern of square paddy parcels for water trapping, with narrow bunds that served as walkways between the lattices. Motorized farming machinery was unable to negotiate this architecture, so water buffalo were used for the plowing of the paddies and all else was done by human hand.

Grain for sowing was always purchased from a trusted source, a farmer of repute. The seeds were primed by sprinkling them with water and storing them in a warm, dark corner of the house until they were just right. Each house had its own corner, which through many seasons of trial and error had proven itself to have just the right combination of light and moisture to allow germination. Tradition dictated that the first handful of seeds be strewn across the fields at an auspicious time, predicted by the right alignment of the planets. This was a ritual to assure the most abundant harvest. There were several astrologers of repute in the village whose sole livelihood was the making of such predictions.

There was nothing my brother and I liked more than to ride with my father to the fields on a Saturday morning. Our car, one of only a few in the village, appeared oddly out of place parked by the fields. There was no greater bliss for a child in those days than to run barefoot through the paddies. We were no exception, but neither was my father. The high point of the expedition was always the moment when we ventured off the walkways and into the muddy parcels themselves, the soft mud extruding through our toes and sinking us, eventually, knee or thigh deep in mud. When inspecting the paddies, my father preferred to dress not in long pants or shorts, but in an ankle-length sarong, easily hoisted up to the thighs and secured around the waist. The farmer who actually worked our paddies lived in a mud-brick hut at the very edge of the fields. In addition to whatever he earned tending to the rice, he also grew a plot of vegetables in a *chena*—an area of dry land—by the side of the fields. His *chena* dripped year round with beans, pumpkins, cucumbers, and gourds. Our household was used to buying vegetables in plastic bags and we found this to be a particularly wondrous sight.

I had never been able to decide when the rice fields were most beautiful. For me, the expectant time was when they were freshly plowed and smelling of stagnant mud. The time of promise was when green fuzz from the young shoots blanketed them. The purely exhilarating time was when ripe golden heads of rice swayed in the afternoon breeze.

Once the rice was sown, there followed tense days until the roots of the already germinated seeds took hold in the soil. Āchchā, my father, and my Uncle Dhaham constantly stared at the sky and wondered if it would continue to rain, allowing the roots to take hold, and if it did, they wondered if too much rain would drown the tender shoots.

When the monsoon left, young grains of rice appeared at the very end of the now tall stalks. Everything turned from green to golden in the relentless sun of the dry season. By this time, the fish that inhabited the rivulets between the paddy parcels and the herons and egrets that fed on them would have long gone, leaving the farmers to contend with the massive flocks of parrots and sparrows raiding the fields. "Thank the gods," my mother often remarked. "It is just the birds here in Depānama and not elephants!" She was making reference to the hazards of rice cultivation in the northern parts of the island, where raids by herds of elephants were a common problem.

Finally, the day of the harvest arrived. It was a day that was prepared for weeks in advance. An auspicious time was again sought for when the first sheaf of rice was severed from the root. Once cut, the sheaves were laid out on gunny mats in the *chena* and trampled by water buffalo until the grains came loose. Mounds of grain were swept into large shallow wicker baskets and held high up against the wind until all the straw blew away. The stones and heavier debris settled on the gunny mats. The skill and experience of the farmer and his helpers was revealed by how clean and yet intact his rice grain became at the end of this process. When properly done, it was only the innermost husk that was left on the grain.

This was the climax of the harvest season. Its success was measured by the count of rice-filled gunny bags available to be transported home, usually by a small tractor and trailer, this being the only use for modern machinery. There were only two such machines to be found in the village. My Uncle Dhaham always had more gunny bags than us to take home. His experience and dedication meant that the ancestral home was always well stocked, with enough excess to sell. My father knew that this was how it should be.

The preparation of the first meal from each new harvest was a special event. The first rice was made into milk-rice. This was a dish prepared by boiling rice in coconut milk until soft and pulpy, and then allowing it to cool to a pudding-like consistency. It was eaten with a savory dish made by combining ground onions and chilies. The making and consumption of milk-rice marked all ceremonial occasions throughout the village, and Kshānti was no exception. It is a heavy meal and induces a state of somnolence only relieved by a long afternoon nap. What better way to celebrate a harvest safe under your roof, meals for the next six months secured, your workers paid, and an overall sense of satisfaction.

There came a time when my brother and I were too old to run among the fields and, just like us, the rice harvest also slowly changed. Fields were not being plowed at every season as they used to be. The village farmers and astrologers were finding work in the city as clerks and peons. For its convenience and taste, my mother had begun to purchase her rice, boiled, husked, and packed in plastic, from a shop in Colombo.

An antiquated way of life that had not only sustained Depānama, but was also the very reason for its existence, was coming to an end. The process of rice cultivation had become too laborious and financially unrewarding. Its traditions had become meaningless.

Before too long, at the insistence of my mother, my father abandoned the fields altogether. His one way of connecting to a place that was not the home he was born in had now become an inconvenience. My Uncle Dhaham, as the head of the ancestral home, held on for longer, but he too would eventually agree with my father, sitting on the veranda at Kshānti, that rice cultivation had become a burden.

The beloved paddies would remain unplowed, overrun with weeds for years. They would slowly suffocate with soil eroded from the surrounding hillocks, from the monsoons which once had nourished them, waiting for a time when they may fill completely and be sold for the construction and industry that was becoming a new way of life for the village.

4

The Gradual New Year

THE NEW YEAR OFFICIALLY ARRIVED in mid-April, but it started to arrive gradually at Āchchā's place from about the beginning of March. The start of New Year season was heralded by the news that new textile material had arrived to the co-op shop, which stood at Junction of the Four Mango Trees on the Borella-Kottāwa Road.

Everyone in Depānama wore new clothes on New Year's Day. In fact, there was no New Year without new clothes. The fabrics had to be purchased and the clothes had to be stitched at least a month ahead. The only outlet from which textiles could be purchased in Depānama was the co-op. The prices were subsidized and the amount available to each household limited to a certain number of yards. The news that the shelves had been restocked at the co-op for the New Year spread like wild fire and a long line of shoppers would form at the Junction of the Four Mango Trees. My Middle Aunt lived at the Junction of the Four Mango Trees and she was able to confirm any news coming from that direction.

Ready-made garments were not available in Depānama those days. Those were only available in Colombo. We were lucky enough to have some of our dresses purchased abroad, and these usually got passed down from the older children to the younger ones. Intimate apparel such as nightdresses, housecoats, underskirts, and petticoats were stitched at home. Of all my aunts, my Youngest Aunt sewed the best. She followed instructions and measurements carefully and kept her stitches neat and tidy. Āchchā was apt at quilting, patchwork, ornate needlework, appliqués, and knitting.

Loud floral patterns in bright bold colors were popular among the women who wore cloth and jacket: Village women wore well-fitting short-cropped jackets with elbow-length sleeves and wrapped the area from their waists to their ankles in several yards of cotton cloth. These garments left the midriff bare. For the New Year, Āchchā sewed nightdresses for us girls and a housecoat for herself. She instructed my Middle Aunt, who was usually charged with selecting the fabrics at the co-op, to buy only pale cottons with dainty designs of flowers, animals, or geometric prints. Sitting on the veranda, Āchchā, my Middle Aunt, and Youngest Aunt unfolded the fabrics, admired the prints, and fingered the cotton. They discussed what to sew, for whom, and how much time they had to get it done.

Soon the staccato buzz of the sewing machine in the front room filled the house. Āchchā's sewing machine was an early model Singer. It had a pattern of flowers and vines painted in gold on its black body and wheel. A foot pedal powered it. Neither Āchchā nor my Youngest Aunt believed in cleaning up as they worked, and when their sewing projects were in progress, the front room became littered with bits and pieces of cloth and string. Cotton fibers became airborne and tickled the nose of anyone entering the front room.

The exchange of gifts was a New Year's tradition. Āchchā worried over what presents to get her grandchildren. "The older children need to get something useful. They can understand things now," said Āchchā. She wanted us to understand that money was important but that it was more important to save it. One New Year she purchased us each a Lucky Card from the post office of Pannipitiya. This was a savings bond that grew in value the longer you waited to cash it. She explained to us that all good things were worth waiting for.

One year my brother and I collected enough money to afford something good enough for Āchchā. We wanted something she would use every day. My mother, who had seen handkerchiefs being sold by pavement vendors in Colombo, decided they would make useful gifts. Each handkerchief was a pastel shade with a scalloped edge. A series of lines at the borders met in a checkered pattern at each of the four corners. The cotton was delicate and the size just right for Āchchā's handbag. Each cost five rupees. Between the two of us we had saved enough for five. We were proud to see Āchchā take our handkerchiefs with her to the post office when she went to collect her pension and to the temple on full moon day.

Sweet meats were made at least a week in advance of New Year's Day, when preparations had reached a frenzied pitch. This was a highly specialized task and required a skilled pastry cook whose skills had been acquired over a lifetime of pastry making. There were only a few cooks of such stellar repute in the village and their services were much sought after during this time of year.

Before the Cook of Sweet Meats arrived at Kshānti, the firewood shed at the back of the house was cleared and a temporary hearth constructed with two separate fireplaces. This arrangement gave the Cook of Sweet Meats plenty of space to work. Each fireplace was made of three bricks that were arranged to surround a fire. Wood for the fire was always gathered from the garden ahead of time. The large frying pans, pots, cauldrons, spatulas, spoons, and molds were taken down from the storage shelves in the kitchen, scrubbed, washed, and made ready for use.

My Uncle Dhaham purchased ingredients needed for the making of sweet meats from Maharagama, such as wheat flour, sugar, and treacle. Coconut milk, grated coconuts, cardamom, cloves, cinnamon, and nutmeg came right from the garden at Kshānti. The rice flour was milled from freshly harvested rice.

When the Cook of Sweet Meats arrived, she was all business. She did not loiter at the Elephant Gates like those who came to pick the flowers from the garden, and she did not linger on the veranda steps like those who came to gossip. Instead, she made her way around to the back of the house. She wore a tight-fitting jacket of white cotton and a flowered cloth from her waist to her ankles. Tucked under her arm she carried a woven reed bag in which she brought an extra cloth to be worn while cooking and the spoons and molds indispensable to her trade. When she arrived at Āchchā's kitchen, she immediately took charge. First, she critically and carefully inspected the cooking utensils and the ingredients Āchchā had laid out for her. She dug her fingers into the rice flour and made sure it had been ground fine enough. She squinted into the wheat flour to make sure there were no mites in it. She dipped her little finger into the treacle and tasted it to make sure no water had been added to it. She checked for mature coconuts by shaking the water inside them. Once satisfied she started mixing the different kinds of dough, batters, and fudge mixtures. Such was her skill that she never used any measuring instrument other than her own two hands.

The Cook of Sweet Meats sat on a low stool at the foot of the fire, fanning and blowing it to life. She pulled at the cloth that covered her legs and adjusted her jacket periodically. She bent over the sputtering coconut oil that was simmering on one fire and dropped a spoonful of batter into it while stirring fudge in a cauldron that rested on top of the other fire. She made sure each cake and biscuit was perfect in size, shape, and consistency and did justice to her reputation.

One by one traditional sweets such as oil cakes, *mung* cakes, *aasmi*, *kokis*, *athirasa*, *aluwa*, and *dodols* got made and assorted on large mats lined with newspaper and left to cool on the dining table. Then Āchchā counted and stored each type of sweet meat in separate metal tins. These were served on New Year's Day, and for weeks after when friends and relatives visited. They were also piled high on platters and sent to neighbors on New Year's Day. The exchange of food platters was a time-honored custom in the village. This practice mended broken bonds, strengthened weakened bonds, and reinforced strong bonds between friends and neighbors.

This time of year fruit trees grew heavy with mango, guava, bell-shaped water apple, *jambu*, and tropical hog plum, *ambarella*. These trees grew tall and bore the sweetest fruit on the highest branches. Birds left the seclusion of the forests and meadows to come to the village to feast on these. "The fruit belongs to the birds," my father said, "it is they who scatter the seed."

If there was a call and sound that was characteristic of this season, it was the call of the cuckoo. The cuckoo was only seen in the village at this time of year. Cuckoos are large birds with a greedy, noisy, and boisterous disposition given to jumping clumsily from branch to branch. The Black-hooded Orioles arrived in pairs and flashed their bright yellow and black on the high branches, and pecked delicately at ripe mangoes and *jambu*. The Ceylon Coucal didn't just stay in the trees. It also liked to hunt for slugs and insects and came down to the ground to look for them. The color of the Paradise Fly Catcher's feathers matched the color of a monk's orange-yellow robe, and in the village it was given the name "Robe-Robber." When its long tail feathers swept across the treetops, it looked like a thief running away, with robes stolen from the clothesline when hung out to dry. Flocks of Green Parakeets with red neck rings arrived to raid the mature rice in the fields.

The most important purchase made during the Gradual New Year was that of the clay pot. The clay pot was required for the making of the first milk-rice of the New Year at the auspicious time set forth and predicted by astrologers. It was a tradition and ritual not only in Depānama, but also throughout the island. It would be the first vessel to be laid on the fire at the dawn of the New Year. From about a month prior to the arrival of the New Year, clay pot vendors set up their wares in makeshift stalls and roadside stands at the Pannipitiya and Maharagama Junctions. The pots they sold were unglazed and matte, orange-brown in color. The surface was cool and granular. The pots were handmade and no two were identical. They came in a few shapes and sizes for the differing requirements of the consumer.

At Kshānti, my Uncle Dhaham selected and bought the clay pot from Maharagama. At the vendor's stand, he first tapped the pot, turning it around and around in his hands to make sure it was of even thickness and evenly fired. He then held it up to the sun and carefully inspected it for holes and cracks. Once he brought the pot home, both Āchchā and my Youngest Aunt repeated the examination by tapping around it and then carefully examining it for holes. Just to make sure no holes or cracks were present, they filled the pot with water and let it sit overnight. A leaking pot placed on the fire on New Year's Day is believed to foretell bad luck to come. It was said that a leak had sprung in the milk-rice pot the year my grandfather passed away.

The gradual New Year would slowly draw to a close at Āchchā's place. The kitchen hearth, quenched of its fire, lay quiescent and cold, cleared of the ashes of the old year and awaiting the sudden arrival of the New Year.

5

The New Year

When the New Year arrived, it arrived suddenly, with a burst of firecrackers from all directions, like rolls of thunder during a monsoon shower. Astrologers predicted the exact time of its arrival many months in advance, so it was not a complete surprise. It is said in ancient chronicles that the sun itself moves from one star formation to another in a yearly cycle. The year commences when the new cycle starts and is celebrated not only in Depānama but throughout the island in mid-April. Before the New Year can be greeted into the home, the old year must be escorted out. Astrologers also predicted the exact time of its departure.

Many of the homes in Depānama consisted of one or two rooms. They were built from clay and repaired about once a year, usually in the weeks leading up to the New Year. Mud floors were smoothed over by the application of a paste made from clay and fresh cow dung. Roofs were rethatched with woven coconut leaves. Our home was built from cement, with concrete floors and clay tile roofing, and did not have this inconvenience. Its French windows opened out on an expanse of well-trimmed lawns on either side of a winding, manicured driveway bordered by lilies. The lilies flowered in April in a profusion of pink, orange, and fuchsia. Our house had the look of newness all year round.

The core of life within any village home, however conveniently or inconveniently constructed, was the hearth. In our home this was a cement shelf occupying about a third of the area of the kitchen. Three separate fireplaces of brick were mounted on the shelf and its smoke directed out through a chimney. To keep tinder such as firewood, coconut leaves, and husks dry, it was stored on a smoking loft mounted over the hearth itself.

The walls of our kitchen were blanketed with soot. Its air was misty with smoke and pungent with the aroma of spices and oils. At no time during the year was the fire in our hearth completely extinguished. Even at night, a few warm ambers were left under the ashes, so that a fire could be started without much difficulty for the morning tea and breakfast hoppers—warm round pancakes with crispy edges and soft fluffy centers.

As a child the kitchen, for me, was a favorite hangout. It was a warm and cozy retreat where keeping company with the cook, the maid, and the gardener was acceptable. Though it could be entered from the main house, those who inhabited this room the most usually entered through the back. Many in the village who visited our home on various errands entered it this way.

I helped our cook sift flour, knead dough, scrape coconuts, mix curries, and ground spices. We used neither electric utensils nor machines in food preparation. Every ingredient used in our cooking was raw and unprocessed, and all subsequent processing done by hand. Planning breakfast started the night before and planning the menu for lunch started as soon as breakfast was cleared off the table.

The kitchen granted its occupants an easy camaraderie and here I heard, without censorship, news of the village brought in through the back door, news of elopements, affairs, and general scandal. My comrades and I huddled together on the low stools that were our only seating and spoke in low voices when we gossiped. Here my brother did not bother me. Here I found escape from the critical eye of my mother. Things tasted better just as they came off the fire, here in the kitchen, and I surreptitiously enjoyed sticky, sweet, hot, spicy, crispy, and oily treats before they reached the table.

For the arrival of the New Year, my mother assumed responsibility of the kitchen, which she otherwise rarely inhabited. Under her direction one of the most inviting rooms in our home assumed an unwelcome sterility. Before the time of expiration of the old year, the hearth was extinguished and cleaned out of all ashes. Our blackened clay pots were scrubbed down. The sooty walls were scraped and whitewashed. Broken utensils were replaced. Spices and grains restocked.

Between the departure of the old year and the arrival of the new, there lay a period of barrenness when the old year had gone and the New Year had not yet come. It was forbidden during this time to light the hearth, start new projects, or engage in any enterprise from which a successful outcome was desired. Stories persisted in village lore of how the mere boiling of a pot of rice or the making of a deal during this inopportune time had led to great tragedy in families. No trader who wished to remain in business traded during this period. No farmer who wished to farm went out onto his fields. No village cook cooked, no seamstress sewed, and no moneylender counted his money. For us, as children, this time seemed to stretch endlessly when we were required to do nothing more than to sit around. In reality, it did not last more than a few hours.

Appropriately it was at the hearth, in the kitchen, where the New Year was welcomed. At the very second that the sun started its new cycle, the matriarch of the home, standing facing a direction advised by astrologers to be lucky, lit a new fire and cooked a new meal of milk-rice.

Everything had to be new. The rice from a fresh harvest, the pot purchased in town, the firewood gathered from the garden, even the clothes worn by all in the home were new.

In our home, my mother always lit the new fire. She was careful to douse the firewood with kerosene oil so it would ignite with a roaring blaze the instant a match was applied. "There," she would say with satisfaction, holding her hands together and closing her eyes in prayer. "May the year that has dawned bring us all good fortune and prosperity."

At this auspicious time there erupted an explosion of firecrackers from all directions in the village. Some from our immediate neighbors were deafeningly loud, others from distant sources nothing more than muffled pops and murmurs. My father would secretly purchase firecrackers from Maharagama a few days before the New Year, when they were abundantly available, and leave them hidden from our mother until this time. For us, as children, and for our father alike, there was no greater excitement than to join with the rest of the village in this cacophony of celebration. Each year my mother discovered the presence of firecrackers and our intent only at the last moment. By this time it was usually too late to object.

My mother always made the milk-rice of the New Year, no matter how much help we had in the kitchen. Once the rice had boiled thoroughly in water, she added the first milk of a freshly-grated coconut and stirred until the rice grains stuck to each other in a milky stew. Then she poured the mixture onto smoked banana leaves and patted it flat. When milk-rice was made in this way, it had a soft, starchy consistency, a strong flavor of coconut, a hint of banana leaf, and a suggestion of the clay pot it was cooked in. "This has come out just right," my mother always commented even before she tasted it. We never disagreed.

The consumption of the first meal, also at an auspicious time, was the next most important task. My brother and I helped lay out our formal dining table in the hall, which was otherwise rarely used. The milk-rice was the centerpiece of our table. It tasted best combined with a dish of sautéed onions, chilies, and dried Maldive fish. The best way to eat it was with your fingers. It was always just the four of us who sat down for the meal, about ten minutes before the appointed time. My mother would switch on the radio. New Year day programming also included announcements of appropriate and opportune times and this helped us keep an accurate schedule. The first bite of the milk-rice would be consumed by my father at the exact moment the time to do so was announced over the radio. My mother, and then my brother and I, followed. This event was also marked by roll upon roll of firecracker blasts throughout the village. The meal at our home was unpretentious. We finished it off with ripe plantains and hot tea. There were times when my mother complained that these traditions were without meaning. My father never worried about the meaning of traditions. He was content that some still persisted in our home.

Later in the day we would meet our aunts, uncles, and cousins at Kshānti, the ancestral home. Before we left our home, my mother gave my brother and I each a crisp new note of rupees. This was her first monetary transaction of the year, and she made it with those she knew would bring her luck.

The meal at Āchchā's place was festive. Plates piled high with sweets: *mung* patties, oil cakes, *kokis*, several varieties of fudge, and chunks of *jaggery*. It never occurred to Āchchā, or to my Uncle Dhaham, who had assumed leadership of the ancestral home, that there was any simpler way to do things other than the way they had been done for generations. It was a day for relaxation at Āchchā's place. My mother and her sisters would retire to the inner sitting room to share stories of their husbands and children. My father and three uncles would sip tea on the veranda and connect over politics, the economy, and the weather. They seldom discussed their spouses or their children, and that may be why they always got on so well. For us, the children, and there were eight of us, there was no greater joy than just being in each other's company.

Our kitchen became a different place when my mother bought a gas cooker. The fireplaces were removed and the hearth tiled with white ceramic. On it was placed the cooker with two burning rings of gas. A rubber hose connected it to a tank of combustible gas. This form of combustion left no residue on the pots and certainly left none to linger in the air or settle on the walls. The chimney was sealed and a new ceiling constructed. Feather-light aluminum saucepans replaced the heavy clay pots. What gas cooking did for food preparation, our new fridge did for food storage. Meals could now be made in a matter of minutes and stored for a whole week.

There was no need now for complex marinades, dry rubs, or for the grinding stone on which they were made. There was no need for freshly milled flour or the wooden flourmill in which it was crushed. Gathering firewood was not a daily chore for our cook. There was more time to gossip now, but we kept our back door closed.

Our relatives marveled at our gleaming kitchen and at how modern and efficient we had become. My mother highly recommended a switch to gas cooking as the initial step to such a transformation, to all those who listened and especially to those who did not.

6

The Four Mango Trees

The Junction of the Four Mango Trees was a crossroad where the Borella-Kottāwa Road met the Cemetery Road and the Avenue of the Brave. Both these roads met the Borella-Kottāwa Road from opposite directions, forming a four-cornered junction. Even though the Borella-Kottāwa Road was the only thoroughfare that ran through the length of Depānama, it was but a lane on which two motor vehicles could barely pass each other. It ultimately connected Depānama to the capital of Colombo through Borella from one direction and through Maharagama via the High Level Road in the other. It was a tarred road, but just barely. When the monsoons came, giant craters opened up along the road exposing the gravel beneath. This was rough on the suspension systems of motorized vehicles, but motorized vehicles were not so common on the roads in those days. This was not such a big problem for the bullock carts and foot traffic.

It was assumed that the Junction of the Four Mango Trees was named for four mango trees that must have grown in its vicinity or thereabouts, but there was no one in the village alive who remembered seeing them there. No one knew of a distant ancestor who claimed to have seen the mango trees at that location either. It may have been named on a whim and not on a natural landmark at all. Somehow the name had stuck. Nonetheless the Four Mango Trees was an important landmark, used frequently by my mother and aunts when directing visitors either to Āchchā's place or ours.

If there was a place that could have been called the center of trade and commerce in the village, it was surely the Four Mango Trees. Yet it held only one place of private enterprise. This private enterprise was the Shop of Hendrick. Its proprietor was named Hendrick. He was also known as the "Pot-Bellied Merchant" and his enterprise also known as the "Shop of the Pot-Bellied Merchant." It was located at the corner of the Avenue of the Brave and the Borella-Kottāwa Road. It consisted of one ill-lit room with an L-shaped counter. Hendrick did all his business from behind this counter and was rarely seen outside of his establishment. His house was connected to the side of the shop. His customers entered his shop and his guests entered his house through the small garden in the front.

Of all those in my family who did business at the Shop of Hendrick, my Uncle Devapiya, the husband of my Middle Aunt, knew him best, as he bought bread for their breakfast each morning from him. The house of my Middle Aunt was next door to Hendrick's house. The two properties were separated by only a few feet of land and a fence. My Uncle Devapiya who preferred to state things simply, if they needed to be stated at all, referred to Hendrick simply as the "Belly." I envisioned a bare belly spilling over from the top of a sarong tied low on the waist, but could go no further as I had never seen him myself.

It was a mystery to many in the village how the Belly flourished from year to year. Flourishing did not imply that he renovated his store, or that he moved into a nicer home, or that he bought a car or motor bicycle, for none of these things happened. He was said to flourish because his store was well stocked, and every few months he added to his inventory of home goods. There was nothing the Belly could not supply. Just as my Uncle Devapiya bought his morning loaf of bread from him, my father bought insecticide and pesticide from him for his rice crops. He sold laundry soap, body soap, coconut oil, kerosene oil, tomatoes, potatoes, and the pots to cook them in. He displayed spices and cereals next to notebooks, pens, and pencils. He sold machetes, spades, and rakes. In the village, he was indeed a capitalist. Towards the Borella side of the Four Mango Trees, there were no shops until you reached the village of Polwatte. Towards the Kottāwa side of the Four Mango Trees, the Pannipitiya Junction was the closest trading post. But not everyone was a fan of Hendrick's capitalism. "He lacks scruples," my Middle Aunt complained many times when she felt she was charged high prices. She may have had socialist leanings, because whenever she could she preferred to shop at the co-op. It was situated diagonally across the junction from the shop of the Belly and offered absolutely no competition to it. The co-op provided the villagers of Depānama with rice and cereals, grains, oil, and textiles at government subsidized prices, and rationed the portions out to each household. A solitary lonesome clerk manned the store when the above items were in stock, but most of the time its shelves were bare and its doors were kept closed.

Trade in the village was by no means an arena confined to men. If there was one woman who dared make that venture a means of livelihood, it was Alice. She did her business out of a window of her house, which in itself could not have been more than two rooms large. Her tiny house-cum-shop was located further along the Borella-Kottāwa Road from the Junction of the Four Mango Trees, on the opposite side of the road from our house and just a stone's throw from our driveway. She had given her boutique a feminine touch by painting it pink on the outside. Alice could not compete with Hendrick at any level, but her little boutique persisted, supported by a few loyal households of which ours was one. She sold bread, sugar-buns, and crocodile-shaped buns twice a day, in the morning and in the afternoon. They were delivered fresh to her shop from the bakery at the Pannipitiya Junction. My mother felt it important to patronize Alice's boutique, and so we bought our bread from her each morning and sugar-buns or crocodile-shaped buns sometimes in the afternoons. Alice could also be counted upon to come to the rescue with the occasional bar of soap or bottle of oil when needed. Despite these frequent transactions, I had never seen Alice. In common with Hendrick, the Pot-Bellied Merchant, she too preferred to do her business in darkness and rarely stepped out of her shop.

If there was one who did his business in the light, it was my grandfather's cousin, Robert. My mother and aunts called him "Uncle Robert." Each afternoon he strolled leisurely down the Avenue of the Brave where he lived, down the Borella-Kottāwa Road, past the front of our house, and into his busy printing shop at the heart of the Junction of Pannipitiya. His shop provided Depānama with all its printing needs, from wedding invitations for private distribution to death proclamations for public distribution. He printed religious books, political pamphlets, and general announcements for circulation. He considered it far nobler to make a living from the propagation of the written word than from trade in vegetables and grain, and so held himself in high esteem. When he took his afternoon stroll to his printing shop, his attitude reflected extreme confidence. He never hurried. He held his head high, his shoulders upright, and clasped his hands firmly behind his back. He smiled, nodded, and exchanged an occasional word with his fellow pedestrians, like a politician on campaign trail. Also like a politician, he wore a spotless white-starched bush shirt and wrinkle-free white sarong. When he stopped at our gate to chat with my father, he spoke with the authority of one who had intimate knowledge of not only village but also world affairs. "I am by all means a capitalist," he proclaimed. "There is no other printing press save mine from Kottāwa to Maharagama." He had expanded upon the wealth he had inherited and now owned several lands, houses, and motorized vehicles.

"Uncle Lewis," as my mother and aunts called him, was also my grandfather's cousin, and he too lived down the Avenue of the Brave. He was a diminutive soft-spoken man who had chosen agriculture as his profession and thus had no need to proclaim his importance. His appearance was curious to us, in that he was one of only two in the village who still combed his hair back and tied it in a little knot at the nape of his neck. It was the style of hair my grandfather too had adopted. The other man in the village who wore his hair long, combed it back, and tied it in a bun was none other than my grandfather's brother, the youngest of his siblings. My mother and aunts called him the "Milk Uncle." He lived at the very end of the Avenue of the Brave, after it wound its way through fields of rice and became all but a narrow gravel footpath. This was where his residential home could be found. He did own a larger home neighboring Kshānti, but this home in interior Depānama is where he kept his dairy of about twenty cows, and from where he distributed milk to his neighbors up and down the Avenue of the Brave. Both Uncle Lewis and the Milk Uncle had inherited their homes and their lands, but neither were capitalists, and neither had expanded upon what they had gained as a birthright.

Buses coming from Borella and Kottāwa made stops at the Junction of the Four Mango Trees several times a day. Those in Depānama who were employed in the outlying towns of Kottāwa, Maharagama, and beyond, and in Colombo, waited here in the morning to catch their buses. They returned in the evening to this junction. This was the transit hub of the working people of Depānama.

Four-cornered junctions where crossroads met were places not only where humans congregated, but where the conditions were just right for dark spirits to congregate as well. At least that was the commonly held belief in those days. Stories would periodically come to light of those crossing the junction at night who had encountered a tall dark woman with long flowing hair, carrying a crying infant and begging for help. Closer inspection would reveal the woman's eyes to be glowing red embers and her cry for help none other than a demonic cackle. But no one who got this close to her lived to tell the tale. It was said they were afflicted with fever, delirium, and eventual death. This specter was the most popular in village lore and undoubtedly the scariest. There were other devilish apparitions, strange lights, and noises said to occur at the Four Mango Trees in the dead of the night. To appease these spirits and ensure the safety of those crossing the junction, offerings of food, flowers, and clay oil lamps were occasionally left by the roadside. Sometimes a small temporary podium would be constructed from young coconut fronds and the offerings placed in it.

Whichever part of the village you lived in and by whatever means you earned your living, it was down the Cemetery Road that all in the village finally traveled. The Cemetery Road was a narrow gravel road that led directly to the only cemetery in Depānama. A stranger to Depānama would not have recognized this piece of land as a cemetery, for it was essentially a bare meadow bordered by rice fields. There were no headstones or burial plots. The grass on it grew tall and free. No walls or fences marked its boundaries. My grandfather had made his final journey to this cemetery, as did his parents before him.

When a funeral took place in the village, the Junction of the Four Mango Trees would be decorated with white flags and light green tender coconut fronds. White was the color of mourning. The corpse would be dressed in white, as would the mourners.

The funeral procession was led by drummers and horn blowers and made its way from the home of the deceased on foot. Once at The Four Mango Trees it turned down the Cemetery Road. Male relatives carrying the coffin on their shoulders followed the drummers. The loved ones, friends, and neighbors followed the coffin somberly. The exuberance of the funeral procession was a reflection of the prominence of the family of the deceased—the more important the family, the more profuse the decorations adorning the roadside, the more numerous the drummers and horn blowers, the louder their instruments, and the longer the line of mourners.

Once the funeral procession reached the cemetery, the coffin would be placed in the middle of a pyre of firewood covered with white cloth, coconut fronds, and flowers. The pyre would be lit at the base by torches carried by male relatives of the deceased. The mourners would watch until the pyre became a spire of fire and smoke.

Once the cremation occurred, the spot was not marked in any way. The following morning the closest relatives would gather at the site where the pyre had stood and collect whatever fragments of bone were visible among the ashes to scatter at a later date, usually in a body of flowing water such as a river or stream. The cemetery was not revisited until the next funeral. We believed that those who had passed from this world and from this life would be reborn in one world or another, in one form or another. Their station in the next life was determined by the sins and merits they had acquired in this life. The cemetery was but a wasteland for the disposal of mortal remains.

7

The Small Harvest

There were many harvests to be had throughout the year in Depānama. The rice harvest was, of course, the most important, but we in Depānama could not be sustained on rice alone. Rice was the main dish, but vegetables were required to be served along with it.

There were two kinds of vegetables: the up-country and the low-country vegetables. The up-country vegetables were grown in the temperate climes of the central hill country and transported by truck to the market in Maharagama. My mother and aunts shopped there once a week, usually on Saturday mornings. Carrots, leeks, cabbage, green beans, and potatoes were the usual up-country fare available at the Maharagama market. These vegetables were mild, and if cooked for too long, they got mushy. They were also more expensive. The consensus in Depānama was that up-country vegetables were an all-around disappointment to grow and eat.

The flavors of the robust vegetables grown in the low-country were enhanced by spices and retained their texture despite prolonged cooking at high heat. These were the ash gourds, bitter gourds, snake gourds, long string beans, pumpkins, melons, okra, and cucumbers. They grew in abundance in the *chenas* of Depānama. *Chenas* were arid plots bordering the rice fields. They were irrigated by rainwater and the runoff from the rice fields, but were not provided with drains and bunds to retain water like the fields were. Only the hardiest of vegetables could still bloom in the scorching sun and stand up to heavy pounding by monsoon showers and bring forth fruit. The rain plumped the vegetables and the sun concentrated the flavors within, and this was why low-country vegetables were so rich and fibrous. In Depānama, what was served at the lunch table was assuredly picked from the vine that very morning. *Chena* crops were sporadic and seasonal. What was grown in the village was consumed in the village. If a farmer was ambitious, he would establish a temporary stall at the Pannipitiya Junction, but he rarely ventured beyond.

Rice and vegetables were obvious necessities and agriculture was a full-time profession in Depānama in those days, but curries and chutneys still needed spices, herbs, and condiments. These were grown in the home gardens of the village. This was the quiet harvest. This was the harvest Āchchā enjoyed the most.

Coffee with its distinctive aroma, potent wake-me-up effect, and nonnative origin was an exotic elixir. The serving of coffee at Āchchā's place was reserved for those occasions when relatives gathered for holidays and ceremonies. Dark coffee heavily sweetened with sugar, served in tiny porcelain cups with matching saucers, and presented to guests at the end of a meal was a tradition at Kshānti.

The coffee served at Āchchā's place was grown in her garden. The coffee grew on bush trees—too tall and sinewy to be called bushes and too frail to be called trees. Its fruit sprouted along the branches. Āchchā had a whole row of coffee bush trees growing along the edge of her property where it bordered the property of her brother-in-law, the youngest brother of her husband. They bore fruit throughout the year. Each morning Āchchā, still in her housecoat, which she wore over her nightdress, strolled along to the coffee bush trees and picked out the ripened coffee fruits. Ripe coffee fruit stood out for its bright red color. Just a handful each time was all there was to be picked.

My Youngest Aunt worried vaguely about Āchchā's morning coffee picking routine. Coffee groves were said to be habitats favored by cobras. My brother and I sometimes accompanied Āchchā on her expeditions, hoping to see a cobra with its hood raised luxuriating in the coffee bush trees, but we had never happened upon one in this state of bliss. The close proximity of the coffee bush trees to the fence separating her property from the property of her brother-in-law posed a diplomatic problem for Āchchā, who held the view that neighbors and relatives should be met mostly at weddings and funerals. She had found this to be the best means of maintaining cordial connections. Āchchā liked to stay true to her views in whatever she did, and so if detained by her brother-in-law or his wife by the fence, she was careful not to exchange anything more than a quick greeting.

The coffee fruit collected each day was left to dry in the sun on a reed mat. Once the fleshy covering of the coffee fruit had shriveled in the sun, Āchchā peeled it off with her nails, exposing the seed-bean within. The naked beans were left to dry some more in the sun and then roasted in a metal pan over the fire. The roasted beans were then pounded by hand until fine and powdery. Āchchā stored her coffee powder in a metal tin. She did not keep this tin in the kitchen. She kept it in her room. Occasionally, when the day had been particularly pleasing or particularly taxing, Āchchā sat on the veranda in the late afternoon and indulged, more or less in secret, in a cup of coffee.

A colossal tamarind tree grew behind Āchchā's house. So gigantic were its branches that it brought shade to the entire area behind the house. It towered over the roof of Kshānti and could even be seen from the front of the house and the road. It was home to scores of squirrels, birds, lizards, geckos, and insects. Scorpions and spiders laid their eggs beneath its thick bark. It layered the ground each day with a carpet of small compound leaves. So massive was its trunk that neither I, nor my brother, nor my cousins, nor even my uncles could wrap their arms around it. It must have been there even before the house of Kshānti was built. This tree was special to Āchchā. For years it had produced gunny bag upon gunny bag of sweet tart tamarind encased in plump woody pods. Each morning, the opening of the back door at Āchchā's place would reveal the fruit of the tamarind fallen all over the ground. Breaking the hard shell of the tamarind pod released the fruit inside. My brother and I preferred to eat tamarind right under the tree that bore it. We combed the ground for the meatiest pod, broke into it, popped the fruit in our mouths, and spit out the seed. We sat on the raised roots of the tamarind and watched each other's faces break out into distorted grimaces when the sour notes of tamarind hit our tongues.

At Kshānti, tamarind pods were shelled, sprinkled with crystals of sea salt, and dried in the sun. Once the sun concentrated the sour elements by drawing out the water, the tamarinds were stored in glass jars. Tamarind added a dimension of acidity to curries, especially fish, jackfruit, and breadfruit curries. Occasionally, when Āchchā was taking her afternoon nap, my brother and I sneaked out and had our fill of dried, salted tamarind right off the drying mats. This was how much we loved tamarind.

The coconut palm is equally useful from root to shoot. The grated flesh of the coconut and the milk squeezed from it were the central ingredients in the preparation of every curry, cereal, and sweet meat prepared in every kitchen in Depānama. Coconut milk could be made savory with the addition of cumin, turmeric, ginger, coriander, and dried chilies. It could be made sweet with the addition of sugar, treacle, or honey. Coconut oil was extracted and used for frying fish, eggplant, and oil cakes. Its oil was also applied to hair to make it shiny and smooth. Its flower was tapped for sap and the sap fermented into an intoxicating toddy. Its large compound leaves were made pliable by emersion in water and used for roof thatching. Its long straight trunk was used for rafters in home building. The little of the palm that was left over was used as firewood.

Though there were regions where coconut was a commercial crop, in Depānama coconut was a household crop. The prosperity of each household in the village could in those days be accurately judged by the count of coconut palms on the property. Āchchā had about two hundred coconut palms on the rear of the property at Kshānti. This was enough to feed not one but ten families and a respectable showing for the household of the widow of the village headman. Every few months, when the heads of the palms had grown heavy with mature nuts and swayed dangerously in the wind, hurling the nuts in all directions, Āchchā decided that it was time to have the coconuts plucked. A message would be sent for the Coconut Plucker.

When the Coconut Plucker arrived at the Elephant Gates, there was never any mistaking who he was. In fact, when the Coconut Plucker walked down the Borella-Kottāwa Road, there was no mistaking his profession. His only attire was a loincloth. The remainder of his slender body he left bare and exposed. His trunk and limbs bore a crisscross of scratches and scars from sliding down the trunks of the palms. He carried a ring made of coconut coir. Standing at the foot of each palm, the Coconut Plucker gazed up into the canopy making a study of the number of mature fruits on each to determine which ones were worth climbing. After passing his feet through the coir ring at the level of the ankles, he would use the ring to hold his feet together to hug the trunk. His feet thus secured, he would hop up the tree as agile as an iguana. One by one, he would yank the mature coconuts off the palm heads and drop them to the ground below. Once one palm was done, he would descend and ascend the next. The Coconut Plucker was the trapeze artist of the village. A man of few or no words, he defied gravity and cheated death every day to make a living. For all his skill and genuine bravado, the fees of the Coconut Plucker were minimal. A single rupee for each palm scaled and as many husked coconuts as he could carry home to his wife was all that Āchchā paid him.

On the day the coconuts were plucked, Āchchā took charge, usually in her housecoat. An unskilled helper hired for the day collected the fallen coconuts and piled them in a mound at the foot of the tamarind. By the end of the day, the mound became a mountain. Āchchā always maintained a carful vigilance over the coconuts from the moment they hit the ground. She counted each as it was piled. The helper husked the coconuts by impaling them on a thick iron rod with a pointed end. From here they were sorted. The best were taken into the house and the others were left out in the shed at the back, where even if a few went missing overnight, no harm would come of it.

A coconut, once husked, is judged for its maturity by holding it up to the ear and shaking it. If the coconut is plump, and if its water sloshes joyously inside, this is a coconut in its prime. Its flesh is firm and its milk is thick and rich in natural oils. If the coconut feels light when held up and empty when shaken, this is a coconut past its prime and plucked too late. A coconut too young to be grated and used for cooking has a bright green husk. This is a *kurumba*. *Kurumbas* are not useful for anything other than immediate enjoyment, and Āchchā allowed only a few to be plucked. The water of the *kurumba* is cool, mild, and sweet. It is best drunk from the nut itself, from a piercing at the top, even before husking. This was how we drank it. The flesh of the *kurumba* scrapes easily off the inside of the shell and is tender and crunchy. We all gathered at the foot of Āchchā's tamarind to drink the *kurumba* water and eat the *kurumba* flesh: my Youngest Aunt, my Uncle Dhaham and their children, my parents, my brother, and sometimes the family of my Middle Aunt. Legend has it that the coconut sprouted from the heavens and that its water is the nectar of the gods. But it was here, in the village, that we coveted and claimed ownership of every palm, used its every part and relished and savored every drop of its sweet water.

8

The Full Moon Day

MANY CENTURIES AGO, RAINWATER MUST have collected in a pool within a depression in an expanse of granite rock about an hour's walk from Depānama. In those days, the journey would also have been made by bullock cart. With the lapse of time, lotus and water lily buds would have arisen from the murky depths of this pool and bloomed at dawn. Small fish, turtles, and tadpoles must have eventually come to call this pool home. As even more time went by, a passing bird would likely have dropped its waste upon this barren rock. The seed of a *bo-fig* tree encased in the droppings must have miraculously laid roots, which snaked through its minutest cracks and crevices to find water and nourishment.

Long ago, a villager living close to Depānama must have stumbled upon this amazing site and come to the obvious conclusion: This was a quiet miracle of nature. This villager must have told other villagers and people from the surrounding villages must have come to see this miracle, and come to the next most obvious conclusion: This was a spot destined for a temple dedicated to the Buddha. A row of rooms for the monks to live in was built along one side of the rock, and a hall for the congregation to gather was built along the other side. A pagoda was constructed in the center and a statue of the Buddha placed in it. Thus was created, long before either Āchchā or I were born, the Temple of Galawila, or the Temple of the Stone Pond.

It was located past Kottāwa, down the High Level Road, about a ten-minute drive from Depānama. Over the years, very little changed at the Temple of the Stone Pond. A system of basic plumbing pumped water into a single faucet that was its only source of running water. For all other needs, water had to be drawn manually from a well. There was a single cable of electricity that powered not more than a couple of light bulbs in the congregation hall. Oil lamps were lit once darkness fell. The accommodations for the monks provided shelter from the sun and rain, but did not house any furniture, such as beds, chairs, or dressers. The monks slept on mats, sat on the floor, and had no possessions other than the robes on their backs.

The full moon day of each month is called the Poya Day. Each Poya has been celebrated for over two thousand years as an anniversary of a significant milestone in the life of the Buddha. It was a special day for us because it was always a school holiday. It was a holiday for my parents, aunts, uncles, cousins, and even for the post office at the Pannipitiya Junction and the shops at the Junction of the Four Mango Trees. It was a day meant to be spent in spiritual reflection. It had always been the practice of people dedicated to the teachings of the Buddha to rest and reflect by spending the day at the temple and observing Precepts of Discipline.

Āchchā and several of her peers chose to observe the Precepts of Discipline at the Temple of the Stone Pond. Āchchā was charmed by the unpretentious and simple observances practiced at this temple. She spent her Poya Day meditating and listening to sermons. For her trip to the temple, Āchchā dressed in a white sari as befitting a lady. The village women usually wore traditional cloth and jacket. Āchchā draped a white cotton shawl across her right shoulder as a symbol of the religious robe, befitting one who observed the Precepts. She took with her a bag that contained a flask of plain tea, a mat to sit on, her pocket radio, and a cup and plate for her lunch.

The Precepts of Discipline required those who chose to observe them to awaken before dawn and adorn themselves with nothing but white clothes that covered the body. They were required to abstain from all contacts that evoked desires. During the course of the day, they sat only on the floor, ate only what was offered to them, and made no demands pertaining to their personal needs or comfort. To spend a lifetime dedicated to such discipline of mind, body, and speech was the path to liberation. This was an austere path in life to follow and a rigorous commitment. This was not for everyone, but one day of each month in such practice was still a step in the right direction. "I will observe the Precepts when I am old and near to death," my mother declared. "I have not the patience for it," she explained. Āchchā had invited me several times to accompany her to the Temple of the Stone Pond, for she knew I was patient, but at that age I lacked the fortitude required to spend an entire day on meditation and inward reflection. I always declined. "Perhaps when you are older," she said. However, that day for us never came.

There were many in the village who lacked patience, like my mother, or who lacked fortitude, like me. Like us, they visited our village temple only in the evening on Poya Day to pay homage to the Buddha. As a family, we managed to visit the temple on at least a few full moon days of the year, though my father would have preferred that we visit the temple at every full moon. On such days, messages were sent to the houses of my aunts, in case they wished to join us. Even after a day of observing the Precepts of Discipline, Āchchā rarely missed an opportunity to visit the village temple in Depānama with us.

Yellow *rukh-aththana* flowers and white *wathu-suddha* flowers were picked from bushes, which like everything else grew in profusion in our garden. We arranged the flowers on wicker platters or piled them into plastic shopping bags. We sprinkled the flowers with cool water to keep them fresh until we placed them at the foot of the Buddha statue in the temple. Passersby on their way to the temple on foot entered our garden looking for fresh flowers. "We are going to the temple ourselves and there is hardly enough for us," said my mother, discouraging anyone from taking our flowers. If we didn't need any flowers, she was even less encouraging. "Flowers are meant to stay on the branches that bore them. The Buddha would not want them dying at his feet," she said.

At the village temple we also lit clay lamps. We made the wicks at home by twisting thin strips, torn from old cotton linens, into cords. Along with cotton wicks, we also took at least one bottle of coconut oil to light the lamps. Cleansing inside and out was one of the objectives of a visit to the temple, and we all washed and donned simple clothes of subdued colors.

The Temple of Parama-Dhamma, which was our village temple, was only about a mile from our home, past the Junction of Pannipitiya, towards Kottāwa, at a minor crossroad known as Moraketiya. This temple had been built many decades ago on a narrow strip of land facing the Old Borella-Kottāwa Road at Moraketiya and, thus, it was also known as the "Moraketiya Temple." The senior monk was elderly and sickly through most of the time I knew him. He was a contemporary of my grandfather and knew Āchchā well. When my mother's attention as a physician was required for the ailing monk, a message would be sent to our home.

Remoteness and sparseness in a temple is conducive to evoking inner serenity in those who visit it. The Temple of the Stone Pond achieved this ambience naturally. The Moraketiya Temple was located at a commercial trade post. It was gloomy and cluttered. Though a wall to shield it from the noise of Moraketiya surrounded the premises, this wall had become derelict with age and was stained and discolored with the growth of green algae. A single-story block of rooms with a small living area and kitchen served as the resident quarters for the monks. This was the "living house." A single light bulb lit the entire building. Kerosene oil lamps were used in the kitchen.

Visitors to this temple, as to any temple, paid homage at three symbolic institutions. First, the *stupa*, a large circular mound over fifty feet in height constructed of cement and brick. Within the inner confines of this structure were said to be enshrined the body relics of the Buddha. We laid flowers, lit clay oil lamps, and burnt incense sticks on the podiums around the base of the *stupa*, as a mark of homage.

The second symbolic institution, the "Buddha House," housed a statue of the Buddha. Prominent temples such as those in Bellanvila and Kelaniya housed not one but many statues of the Buddha in different postures in a group of connecting shrine rooms. The temple at Moraketiya had but one statue in the sitting posture in a single shrine room. It is customary for the walls of the shrine room to be decorated with murals from the life and time of the Buddha. The walls of the shrine room at the Moraketiya Temple were decorated with graphic, frightening murals of devils, demons, and bandits who were calmed in the presence of the Buddha. Once we had offered flowers at the Buddha statue, my brother and I did not linger admiring the murals or walking around the shrine room, as we did at Bellanvila or Kelaniya.

Behind the Buddha House at the very back of the premises was the *bo-fig* tree. The Buddha is said to have attained enlightenment while meditating under the shade of a *bo-fig* tree. This is the third symbolic institution of significance at a temple. As with every temple, an ornate barricade was constructed around the *bo-fig* tree at Moraketiya, but as with everything else at Moraketiya, it was stained green with mold and algae.

On the day the older monk passed away, my mother was called to his side. My brother and I sat with our father in the old wicker chairs in the living room of the resident quarters and peered into his dark room as he moved in his bed restlessly. That day the temple was even darker and gloomier than before. All of Depānama and many hundreds of monks attended his elaborate funeral. With the passing away of the elder monk, a new era dawned in the temple at Moraketiya, just as a new political era had dawned in the village with the passing of his contemporary, my grandfather. The young junior monk assumed the position of leadership at the temple. He was educated at the University in Colombo and his habits were those of the city. He stubbornly named the Sunday school the "Celsius College," which was puzzling to the village elders. He started handicraft programs and math and science classes for youth. He disliked long ceremonies and looked for ways to cut them short. He discouraged elaborate rituals. His youth and familiar attitude when addressing his congregants made Āchchā uneasy. She was used to serious dialog with the older monk, and the light-hearted banter of the new monk put her off. Gradually our visits to the temple at Moraketiya lessened.

The most special Poya Day of all is the full moon day in the month of May. This Poya marks the birth, enlightenment, and the passing away of the Buddha and is given the name "Vesak Poya." Vesak is a celebration of lights. On this night, and for two nights thereafter, every garden in the village is decorated with flags, lanterns, candles, and lamps.

Just as with any other celebration in the village, preparations start long before the day itself. Village youth made elaborate, three-dimensional geometric lanterns in the shapes of hexagons, octagons, and lotus blossoms using dwarf bamboo sticks tied together with rubber string. There were many youth in Depānama highly skilled at lantern making and their creations were admired throughout the village. Once the framework was made, the sides were covered with brightly colored tissue or wax paper. On Vesak Night, these lanterns were hung from the branches of trees, on porches and verandas. Candles and coconut oil lamps lit within them scattered colored light in all directions. Occasionally, one of these intricate and painstakingly created works of art would sway in the wind, catch fire from within, and burn down, as if illustrating the impermanence of life itself and the eventual fate of the body we inhabit.

My brother and I had no skill in lantern making. We had tried many times, but had failed in the early stages. Buckets were sold at the Pannipitiya Junction in the weeks leading up to Vesak. Buckets were for those of us who did not know how to make lanterns. A bucket had the shape of a small beach bucket and was made of a circular cardboard base surrounded by colored wax paper on the sides. There was a single mount within the base of the bucket to hold a candle. They were sold by the dozen and my mother usually bought about four dozen, enough for our whole garden.

On Vesak Day my father hung crisscrossing rows of flags all across our garden. On Vesak Night my father lit the candles and affixed them to the inside of the buckets carefully. My brother and I hung them on low-lying branches and bushes on our lawn. After the work was done, my parents, brother, and I walked up and down our driveway admiring the effect of so many brightly colored lights flickering and shimmering in the darkness of Vesak Night. Many in the village walked along the Borella-Kottāwa Road on their way to the temple and stopped by our gates admiring our work. My father had purchased a row of electric bulbs on one of his trips abroad and he hung them over our balcony. This was a time when colored electric bulbs were rarely available, and we were proud to have our own row of lights to compensate for our lack of lanterns. The roads around Depānama were busy on Vesak Night. People took to the roads by foot and in motorized vehicles to see the sights and enjoy the sounds. Soft drinks and meals were distributed free of charge from large roadside tents put up specially for feeding thirsty and hungry sightseers. Traffic slowed down. The police station at Maharagama dispatched several of its officers to keep the peace and ensure safety. Both Kottāwa, to one side of Depānama, and Borella, to the other, boasted giant Vesak *pandols*. A *pandol* was a mural lit with many thousands of electric bulbs sometimes synchronized to turn on and off to music, depicting a story from the life of the Buddha. They were many stories high and drew hundreds of people to Borella and Kottāwa on Vesak Night.

The dry season lasted from the New Year in April to the Poya of Vesak in May. The rice fields at this time were dry, cracked, and parched. Each afternoon we carried buckets of water drawn from our well to water the flowering plants in our garden. The water level in our well became low, exposing the spring that supplied our household with water nearly seventy feet beneath our property. Our electric water pump could not draw water from this depth and we were without running water in our bathroom and kitchen at this time of year. We took our baths and washed our clothes by the well. It was as if the village was stuck in limbo, in the grip of a dry and humid spell cast over it by Mother Nature herself. The night of Vesak was also the night when the first showers of the Southwest monsoon hit landfall, bringing with it rolls of thunder, streaks of lightening, gusts of winds, and sheet upon sheet of dense life-giving rain. In a matter of a single night, the fields would flood, green grass shoots would sprout, and the spring in our well would once again become submerged with fresh, naturally filtered water.

9

Little Lady

Podi hamine, meaning little lady, was how Āchchā addressed her second daughter. "She was a beautiful child," Āchchā said. "Her face was even rounder and her hair was even curlier than now." We all believed that my Aunt Indi must have been a beautiful child, for how else could she have grown up to be such a beautiful aunt? There was a single photograph in the possession of my Youngest Aunt that attested to this fact. In black and white it showed my aunt as a toddler of perhaps two, in a baby-doll dress, shoes, and socks. She was giving the camera a sour look, but still looked cherubic doing it. But how, I wondered, did she acquire so much sophistication? Had she not grown up in Depānama?

From a young age, Āchchā told me, her second daughter had an appreciation of the finer things. She was particular, said Āchchā, not only about her outer dress but also about her petticoats. She was the first of Āchchā's daughters to cut her hair short. She styled it to frame her face and emphasize its natural curl. She complimented her peach complexion with blush-pink lipstick and rouge. These were her natural sensibilities. She must have been naturally inclined, then, to fall in love with my Uncle Winston when they met, while they were both still in school. He was tall, slim, confident, and just as sensible to the perception of perfection as was she. He was the youngest male in a large family, and upon their marriage, my aunt moved to live with him in his ancestral home, in a town in the district of Kaluthara. He and his extended family owned several estates of tea, rubber, and rice. They engaged in industry in ready-made garments, textiles, batiks, and raw rubber for export. They were not only intimate with the higher echelons of Colombo society, they were a part of it. Like a hand sliding into a well-fitting glove, my Aunt Indi had eased into a life that suited her imminently, or so it seemed to us.

My Aunt Indi was accustomed to shopping at the exclusive boutiques in Colombo for her clothes. Having no dress code to follow, as did my mother and Middle Aunt in their respective work places, she was not restricted to the sari as the staple in her wardrobe. She was free to accommodate the dictates of the latest in Western fashion. She frequented beauty parlors patronized by the movie stars, she said. Her creams, facial foundations, and powders had to be Revlon, a brand highly coveted and not freely available at the time. Her eyeglasses had to be Ray-Bans. She and my Uncle Winston received invitations to the homes of prominent politicians. When they threw parties at their own home, it was for this class of honored guest. My aunt attended coffee mornings, fashion parades, plant shows, and fundraisers with city socialites to fill the void caused by the lack of the daily grind. Though we traveled daily to Colombo for school and work, our base was securely in the village and we had no part or place in the life that belonged to my Aunt Indi. We knew of these things only because she told us about them.

The traits of my Aunt Indi, had they been present in anyone else, would have caused alienation from Kshānti. In her case, they only resulted in endearing her more to those from her childhood home. Her personality was effusive and vibrant. If she was expected at a family gathering at Kshānti, the expectation was palpable, and if she failed to turn up, the disappointment was bitter. She was self-assured when she entered a room and warm and welcoming when she greeted those in it. She engaged everyone in conversation, from her relatives to the cooks and maids, with equal familiarity. So, rather than begrudge her the effortless glamour she lived in, we sought to share in it through the stories she told us. She had the knack of holding her audience captive with vivid descriptions of the grandeur and splendor of weddings, banquets, dinners, and dances she had attended. She had close knowledge of illicit liaisons of the rich and famous and could report on them more colorfully than a society columnist employed by the *Daily News*.

My mother viewed life with a great deal of seriousness and disapproved of the gaiety with which my Aunt Indi treated it. She delighted in seemingly frivolous things and had the gift of imparting the delight she felt to those around her. Āchchā loved this about her. It was probably the reason why she looked forward to her visits so much. "You are so fond of her only because you see her less," my mother said of her sister to Āchchā, annoyed. If my mother had a sibling whose characteristics were a direct contrast to her own, then that sibling was my Aunt Indi. Contrast and contradiction were bothersome to my mother in general and these characteristics in my Aunt Indi she found to be exceedingly so. If we thought the life of my Aunt Indi was charmed, my mother thought it completely wasted. My Aunt Indi had studied for and obtained a university degree from one of only two universities in existence at the time. This was a testament to her intelligence. She had chosen homemaking over a career, when it was my mother's opinion that she could have had and excelled at both, as she believed herself to have done. My mother saw my aunt as taking the easy way out and for this she scorned her.

When addressing each other in public, my Aunt Indi and Uncle Winston did not use their names, but a term of endearment that they had coined. My mother found this to be an embarrassment. The outward display of affection is a sign of inner turmoil, she maintained. In an effort to dispel any hint that her own marriage was afflicted by inner turmoil, my mother addressed my father in stern and severe terms, in a tone similar to the one she used for us, her children. If this were not enough, my mother said the gift-giving habits of my Aunt Indi were wasteful. My aunt gave generously and thoughtfully.

I had known this aunt all my life. Yet, my feelings for her were based on observations of what she allowed me to see of her rather than on an understanding of who she was. I cherished the close, affectionate relationship I shared with my Youngest and Middle Aunts. There was an inner vulnerability to each that neither had hidden from me, even as a child. Of my own vulnerabilities they knew more than I did myself, having had a hand in raising me from the very time of my birth. My regard for my Aunt Indi was not based in the mutual sharing of our imperfections, but rather upon my need to believe in her veneer of perfection. As I grew older, my belief in the external veneer faded and eroded. Though I searched for an underlying fondness, forged by the bonds of blood and family to replace it with, I could not find it.

My Aunt Indi was mother to two girls born a year apart; the older, and my favorite cousin growing up, was only a year younger than me. We traveled to visit them every few months, usually on a Saturday afternoon. My father would drive for an hour on winding narrow roads through fields of rice and rubber to reach their home. Their home was the ancestral seat of the family of my Uncle Winston and bore every indication of this distinction. It was located in the center of a property that also housed a shed for the cows at the back and a weaving mill on the side. The house had many rooms with elaborately carved doorways and narrow inset windows, which let in very little natural light. To my young mind, its dim hallways suggested the persistent presence of distant ancestors. Adding to this effect of having stepped into a dark past was the aging father of my Uncle Winston, a tall, lanky, forbidding figure who held his sarong up with one hand and swayed slowly from side to side as he walked. His mystery was deepened by a story my cousin had told me of how her grandfather kept the hairs of a dead elephant in a pot beneath his bed. The elephant had been one of several he owned, and it had collapsed and died of a heart attack in the middle of town many years ago.

At dusk, an electric generator would start up with a low rumble from some inner recess of the house, and weak flickering bulbs would come to life with an eerie glow. However hospitable our aunt and uncle had been to us, and however much fun we had had with our cousins, this was our cue to leave, and we couldn't wait to get back to Depānama.

The arrival of my Aunt Indi and cousins at Kshānti for visits was an event much looked forward to by my Youngest Aunt and Āchchā. Their arrival was announced to the household by the toot of their car horn at the Elephant Gates. My aunt and uncle bought new cars frequently, and we looked forward not only to seeing them, but also to the car they travelled in. At various times they had owned a jeep and also a pickup truck. My uncle tooted the horn at the Elephant Gates to make sure someone was home, even though someone was always at home at Kshānti. At the urgency of this sound, my Youngest Aunt would run to the Elephant Gates and hurry to open them. Rolling down the shutter, my Aunt Indi would call out to her sister, "Little One! We have to go soon!" indicating that this was not a long visit and that her time was precious.

When we had admired and complimented her on her attire and accessories and when she in turn had informed us of their expense and exclusivity, the preliminaries were done. She never came empty-handed. She always brought with her something good for Āchchā and us: pastries, cakes, sweet and savory treats. Most often she would bring an ice-cold block of fruit-and-nut ice cream from the Elephant House Ice Cream Shop at Maharagama. She would hand it over to my Youngest Aunt as soon as she entered the house, to be served and shared right away for immediate enjoyment and instant gratification.

My Aunt Indi would eventually settle down, as did everyone else sooner or later, in an armchair on the veranda to gossip. Often, at the urging of my Youngest Aunt, she would retell a tale from the village from the time when she and her sisters were children when their father was still alive. These were legends well-known in the family for having been told many times before. In her storytelling she gave new life to people and places long since gone, as if it had been but yesterday. Then at the end would come the line that made the whole story funny or poignant, and the veranda would resonate again with roars of laughter as it must have done again and again all those years ago.

Tales told and treats gone, it would be time for my Aunt Indi to leave. Āchchā said goodbye to my aunt from the veranda, but we went right to the Elephant Gates. Not wanting to let her go, we would cling to the gates, peering and waving through the ironwork until her car disappeared around the bend, away from Kshānti.

10

The Middle Aunt

I KNEW ĀCHCHĀ'S THIRD DAUGHTER, my Middle Aunt, faced more hardship in life than did Āchchā's other daughters. "It is a way of life of her own choosing," my mother told me. Rather than agree to a proposal of marriage arranged by Āchchā, to a family of means and prominence, she had fallen in love with a young man who was to later become my Uncle Devapiya. She had chosen him for her mate and married him in secret while still living under her mother's roof. She left Depānama in disgrace on the day her marriage was discovered, when my Uncle Devapiya turned up at Kshānti to claim her for his wife. She had taken nothing with her when she left to live with him and his relatives in a distant town in the district of Ratnapura, at least an eight-hour journey from Depānama. The shock to those at Kshānti must have been tremendous and the scandal hard to live down in a village where everyone else's business was your own, and your own business was the business of everyone else. "Thank the gods," Āchchā had told me, "your grandfather had already passed and was not alive to witness it." That was all she said about it.

It was a departure from the way marriages were conducted in those days. There was no negotiation of dowries, no formal visits between the families, no matching of wealth, reputation, and education. There was no wedding.

There followed a period of estrangement between the family at Kshānti and my Middle Aunt. Her new relatives welcomed her when those at Kshānti shunned her. When she first arrived in her husband's home, they arranged for her to be dressed in a wedding sari and veil, and a formal photograph of the new couple was taken at a studio in town. It did not have the polish of one taken at Donald's, the premier studio in Colombo, where all the wedding photographs of Āchchā's daughters were taken, but it was all that could be done under the circumstances. When she soon became pregnant with her first child, her in-laws cared for her through her confinement. So Rashmi, her first daughter, was born in the hometown of my Uncle Devapiya.

Time and the arrival of Rashmi, Āchchā's fifth grandchild, must have healed old wounds. When Rashmi was still a toddler, Āchchā welcomed her third daughter back to Depānama. I don't know if my Middle Aunt ever asked Āchchā for her forgiveness for the heartache she had caused her, or if Āchchā had forgiven her without being asked. I also don't know if Āchchā had asked forgiveness from her daughter for trying to force her into a marriage that she did not want. It was symbolic of forgiveness, however, that Āchchā allowed the photograph of my Middle Aunt and Uncle Devapiya, taken upon their marriage, to be displayed on the cabinet in the living room at Kshānti along with the wedding photographs of her other three daughters. It stood out from the rest for its starkness. It was forgiveness that mended the bond broken by their mutual betrayal.

My Middle Aunt settled down in a small house right in the heart of the Junction of the Four Mango Trees with my Uncle Devapiya and my young cousin. The house and land were a gift from Āchchā. It was a good place to raise a family, and my Middle Aunt must have been grateful for Āchchā's gesture. The house had but a single bedroom, a loft, a small living room, and kitchen. Later, a second bedroom, dining area, and a bathroom were added. The land was a narrow strip along the Borella-Kottāwa Road and permitted no further construction.

My Middle Aunt and Uncle Devapiya travelled by bus most of the time. She had no maids, cooks, or gardeners to help her run her house. There was no need for it. She did not have the distinction of living in the ancestral house, as did my Youngest Aunt, or the distinction of being the eldest daughter of the former village headman, as did my mother, and so no appearances to keep up. Hers was a hard won freedom from the confines of tradition, but her domestic hardships may have obscured her view of freedom.

My brother and I spent a great deal of our childhood in the company of our cousins, who became as close to us as siblings. The first daughter of my Middle Aunt especially so, given that our home was only two houses down from theirs, and both these homes only a half mile down the road from Kshānti.

Rashmi, my Middle Aunt's firstborn, was an only child for five years before her sister and the last of Āchchā's grandchildren were born. The children of my Aunt Indi were closer to us in age and temperament and we would have liked to have their company everyday, but they lived more than an hour away and we did not meet with them more than once or twice a month. Rashmi was our daily companion. Rashmi was always ready and eager to join in any game of our choosing. She was an energetic child whose thirst for exploration and excitement tired us with its excess. She was good for rough and tumble games, and we were glad to have her as a playmate when we were in the mood for such. When it was time to go in the house, get cleaned, and sit down with a book, she was no good. She was no good for serenity and quietness. We were older and yet could not tame her.

When we played hide-and-seek, she would find a deep ditch with tall weeds to hide in, where bites from mosquitoes, if not poisonous snakes, were all but a certainty. If she climbed a tree, she would chose one from which she could not climb down. When playing hopscotch, she would land on all fours instead of on one leg. She ate wild berries without telling any one of us, just to check if they were edible. She wasn't careful when exploring the garden and rubbed her limbs against itchy poison creepers. On most days, she would scrape her knees and elbows on rocks and tree trunks and, if indoors, she would bounce her head on furniture and get her fingers caught between doors and windows.

This precious child of my Middle Aunt was said, on good astrological authority, to have been born with the prevalence of Saturn as her ruling planet and, thus, was prone to ill fate as a youngster. Her perplexing nature and her distressing tendency to inflict herself with bodily injury was no fault of her own. It simply was the influence of the wicked planet Saturn. This was the widely held belief in the family. Saturn was not a kind patron and could even inflict sudden and instantaneous death upon its subjects. To protect her child from the malefic influences of Saturn, my Middle Aunt hung a *yantra*, a small barrel-shaped gold pendant, around Rashmi's neck. Inside the pendant, engraved on thin sheets of copper, were symbols and stanzas with protective powers from the ancient scriptures. There were times when this was not enough, and an additional *yantra* would need to be tied around her waist and holy strings blessed by ritualistic chanting at the temple tied around her wrists.

It was mostly during the school holidays that my brother and I spent time at Kshānti, in the charge of my Youngest Aunt, in the company of Āchchā. Growing up, my Youngest Aunt became a second mother to me and, as I grew older, I found in her a loyal friend and confidant. Rashmi joined us at Kshānti. My Middle Aunt dropped her off in the morning.

My Middle Aunt arrived at the end of the day to collect my cousin. She took the bus from her workplace and it stopped right in front of the Elephant Gates. It was not her style to step quietly inside. Instead, she rattled the latch, shouting from the street to my Youngest Aunt, "Little One! Little One! Open the gate, will you!" Rushing onto the veranda, she would head straight for one of the armchairs and slump into it. Pushing her feet out from under her sari, she would stretch her legs and inhale deeply. This was a sign that her workday had been hard and long. The journey from her workplace in Colombo to Depānama took at least an hour by several buses and left the traveler grimy with dust and sweat. To show us that this was indeed the case, my aunt would twist about in her chair, whip up the end of her sari, and wipe her face with it.

My Youngest Aunt, by the luxury of the good position held by her husband, had no need to work. She must have felt apologetic and, perhaps to sooth her own discomfort as well as the obvious fatigue of my Middle Aunt, offered her tea. Sometimes she would go so far as to get her biscuits or cake, depending on what was available in the house. My Middle Aunt would accept what was given to her distractedly. Preoccupied with her own thoughts, she offered her younger sister a smile. At these times, my Middle Aunt had the victorious attitude of one who had done battle not only with corporate overlords, but also with the public transportation system, and lived not only to tell the tale, but to fight another day. To her, the armchair on the veranda was not just a chair, but a throne.

Settled on her throne, she beckoned her daughter to come to her. Her shrill call of "Rashmeee! Rashmeeeee!" would echo through the living room, down the hallway, past the dining room, into the kitchen, and towards the garden at the back. "It is an eagle calling for its chick," my father had commented once, with his gentle humor. When her offspring appeared, usually reluctantly from the recesses of the ancestral house and grounds, my Middle Aunt would pull the child towards her, first peering into her eyes, then examining her limbs for scratches, scrapes, and bruises, and finally running a quick hand over her head checking for bumps. Still not satisfied, she would demand of my Youngest Aunt, "Did she hit her head?" This ritual exemplified the perpetual anxiety that my Middle Aunt suffered on behalf of the well-being of her child. It was attributed again to the evil threat of Saturn upon the health and safety of my cousin. Both Āchchā and my Youngest Aunt understood and were empathetic. They had learnt on these occasions to keep silent.

Finally, my Middle Aunt would sigh. It may have been a sigh of resignation. Her sudden realization that even at the end of a long work day and an exhausting journey home there now awaited the preparation of the evening meal, the cleaning of the pots and pans, the turning in for the night, and the inevitable necessity of having to do it all over again the next day. My Middle Aunt would hurriedly depart through the Elephant Gates, Rashmi's small hand gripped tightly in hers, pushing her away from the road and towards the gravel curb as they made their way home. We would watch Rashmi, who would turn to wave at us again and again, until she rounded the bend leading away from Kshānti, her scamper halted sometimes as she kicked a stone or inspected an insect. Her eyes closed with head thrown back, Āchchā would lean a little further in her armchair on the veranda. It was now her turn to sigh.

II

Forbidden Fruit

WHEN ALLOWED TO GROW in the sun and ripen, most tropical fruit became soft and intoxicatingly sweet. When we were young, we craved unripe fruit while still crunchy, sour, and acidic. Our mother had forbidden the eating of unripe fruit. She warned that the acid would numb our teeth and sour our throats.

Luxuriant tropical fruit trees grew riotously in the compound at Kshānti. They had all been planted many decades earlier by the family of my grandfather or by Āchchā while she was still a newlywed, also many decades ago.

Of all the fruit-bearing trees in Āchchā's garden, the *jambu* was her favorite and ours too. *Jambu* is a small, mildly sweet fruit shaped like an upside down hot air balloon. The smallest of the three trees on Āchchā's property stood just outside Āchchā's room. When the *jambu* was plentiful, it was almost possible to reach the low branches and pluck the fruit through her window. Though Āchchā rarely tasted the *jambu*, she was protective of this tree and possessive of the fruit it bore for the vibrant spectacle it made when in season. *Jambu*, in varying stages of ripeness, ranged from a pale pastel pink to a bright glaring red. To complement this color palette, the leaves of the tree were a brilliant green. The visual impact was as stunning and as glorious as any Vesak *pandol* on the full moon day of May. Squirrels and birds fed on the clusters of fruit throughout the day. We were children and only vaguely aware of this wonder of nature. We were more interested in the taste of ripe *jambu.*

The best time to get at the *jambu* outside Āchchā's window was when she retired for her afternoon nap. Crouching low against the wall outside her room, my brother and I would first listen for the sound of her snoring and then peek over her windowsill into her room as she lay on her bed, to make certain she was asleep. Careful to crackle as few leaves as possible, we crept up to the tree like a pair of cat burglars. We could not always reach the best fruit by standing tiptoe and, therefore, had to resort to throwing stones to get it to fall. We selected a few stones likely to inflict the most damage. My brother, who could throw higher and with much better aim than I could, made the attacks, while I kept watch on the sleeping figure of Āchchā.

Jambu does not need to be peeled. If it does not hit the ground, it doesn't even need to be washed. The flesh around the fuzzy seeds is as crisp as the flesh of a cucumber. The best condiments to eat fresh *jambu* with are a few grains of salt and peppercorns. When the Depānama Junior School, two doors down from Kshānti, let the children out in the early afternoon, little boys and girls squeezed in through the fence and entered Āchchā's garden, surreptitiously looking to attack the *jambu* tree. They were more in number and made more noise than we did, but they were also more skilled at throwing stones and made off with more loot than us, if Āchchā didn't shoo them off first.

Just as Āchchā was proprietorial about the *jambu* outside her window, my Uncle Dhaham was proprietorial about the *ambarella* tree outside his window on the opposite side of the house. Its ovoid fruit, which hung in large bunches, was the size of a small guava, and its flesh surrounded a coarsely fibrous seed. Each time the wind shook the high branches, it caused the heavy fruit to fall onto the roof with a loud thud. The meat of the *ambarella* was firm and tart when raw, sweet and fibrous when ripe. My Uncle Dhaham especially liked the curry made from raw *ambarella* fruit, cooked down with spices and coconut milk and eaten with rice and dried fish. He had forbidden the throwing of sticks and stones at the *ambarella* tree and would regard us with suspicion if he found us anywhere near it. The *ambarella* tree was taller than the house and spread its canopy of branches well over the side of it, jostling for space with the fan-like leaves of the coconut palms and the branches of the massive mango trees that gave that side of Āchchā's garden a dark and forbidding gloom. An open drain, emptying the bath water from the house, ran across this side of the garden, and the shade of the trees stopped the moisture from lifting, even on the sunniest of days.

This side of Āchchā's garden bordered the compound of her brother-in-law, the younger brother of my grandfather. The dense growth of tall trees and lush underbrush secluded Kshānti from its immediate neighbors on this side, a situation both Āchchā and my Youngest Aunt preferred. "After all, we meet at weddings and funerals," was the policy Āchchā maintained. Āchchā's brother-in-law was the only male sibling of my grandfather still alive at the time of my birth. My mother and aunts called him the Milk Uncle as he owned a dairy of a few cows. My brother and I did not know what to call him and seldom addressed him directly. He looked very much like the large picture of my grandfather that hung at Kshānti. "The Milk Uncle looks so much like your father," I had commented to my mother, when old enough to observe the similarities. "Not at all," replied my mother, hinting at some old underlying discord. "Our father's face was round and very fair. He was distinguished in looks as well as in station."

"Of course the Milk Uncle got around the village as a lad," said my Youngest Aunt, adding fuel to the fire. "Why, that is how he met the Little Mamma." The "Little Mamma" was the Milk Uncle's wife. She must have been petite and pretty in those days, and she still was in the days when I knew her. I came to know that the liaison had been forbidden because her station in life was beneath his. "After all, she was only just from the village," my Youngest Aunt explained, exposing hidden prejudices.

When the Little Mamma stepped in to visit Āchchā for a chat and a cup of tea, she did not sit on the veranda step as the other village women did, but neither did she sit on the big armchairs as my aunts did. Instead she sat on a set of low straight chairs facing Āchchā. Even though she addressed Āchchā as she would an elder sister-in-law, she bowed her head slightly when doing so. She was careful to always keep her feet tucked in under her chair and her arms folded neatly on her lap.

A troop of black monkeys roamed the village across the treetops from one end to the other. They jumped, hopped, swung, and catapulted from the crowns of the coconut palms to the peaks of the rubber and jack trees. If they couldn't make a crossing among the trees, they got on the rooftops. They were a rowdy bunch, headed by a few large dominant males. The babies clung to the underbellies of their mothers as they swung through the canopy. Once high off the ground, the babies left the safety of their mothers and practiced their acrobatic moves playfully. My mother thought the monkeys were a nuisance. When they got on our roof, they cracked and broke the clay tiles. We found out about it only when the dry season came to an end and the rains came. The broken tiles made it rain inside the house almost as much as it did outside the house. We ran about placing pots, pans, and basins throughout our rooms and living room to catch the rainwater. My mother had our father go up on the roof and replace broken tiles periodically. Eventually fed up, she cut the trees down around the house to stop the monkeys from jumping onto our roof.

The monkeys had a habit of raiding the banana plants, the mango, the *ambarella*, and the *rambutan* trees when they were in season. If the fruits they plundered were ripe, they ate the meaty parts. If they found the fruit too young and sour and didn't like how it tasted, they threw the half-eaten fruit onto the ground. When the troop visited our garden and behaved in this unruly way, my father was generous and indulgent. "What grows on the trees belongs to the animals first," he said. "They must have their fill before we can." Sometimes they pulled off young coconuts when only just buds and threw them down just for fun.

My Uncle Dhaham was not like my father, and these wasteful antics infuriated and annoyed him. When the troop entered the compound at Kshānti looking for a feast, he sprung into action immediately. He hurried through the hall to the back of the house shouting out to my Youngest Aunt, "The monkeys are here! The monkeys are here! Get the firecrackers! Get the crackers out!" He kept a store of firecrackers, usually left over from the New Year festivities, just for this purpose. He positioned himself strategically, like a sniper looking for the perfect vantage point, and lit and threw the firecrackers into the treetops. With the first explosion, pandemonium broke out as the startled troop scattered in fear for their lives. They would flee Āchchā's garden in a matter of a few scurried seconds, the mothers gathering up their babies and tucking them under their bellies, the juveniles jumping onto the taller coconut palms for cover. Though my Uncle Dhaham always insisted that no harm was caused by his deterrent methods, we were not so sure. Certainly no primate with a weak heart or a shaky nervous system could possibly survive such a scare, we thought.

At the end of fruit season, when my Uncle Dhaham had had enough of the squirrels, monkeys, school children, nephews, and nieces getting at the trees, when the ground was littered with discarded seeds, and when the fruit flies buzzed in his ears every time he stepped outside the house, he decided it was time to strip the *ambarella* and mango trees bare. A long bamboo pole that reached to the very top of the coconut trees, twice as high as the roof, would be fetched and a steel hook attached to its end with coir string. Peering at the treetops with the bamboo waving perilously in his hands, he would take aim at bunches of *ambarella* and mango. He hooked each bunch and tugged sharply, causing a hail of fruit. We all watched anxiously from a safe distance.

When this dangerous activity was over, Āchchā and my Youngest Aunt set to work storing the semi-ripe mangoes and *ambarella* in large cardboard boxes between sheets of newspaper. To hasten maturation, these boxes were stored in the rice bin, a large square wooden box used for storing rice that occupied about a quarter of the space of Āchchā's kitchen. Its warmth and humidity promoted the conversion of acids into complex sugars, sweetening the fruit. In our opinion, to sweeten any fruit was to waste it. Tropical fruit was best eaten peeled, when still raw, ground lightly on a grinding stone and pickled with salt, pepper, chilies, and vinegar. My brother, my cousins, and I dished our pickled fruit into empty coconut shells and sat on the low wall at Kshānti, our legs dangling over the side, looking out over the Borella-Kottāwa Road. This was by far the best way to enjoy anything forbidden.

12

The Fishmonger

MEAT AND FISH WERE DELICACIES in the village in those days. These sources of protein were not always available and, even if available, too expensive to be affordable on a daily basis. Parents bought these items for their growing children when they could, but went without for themselves. When visiting the sick and the ailing, relatives brought curries of fish and meat to help with the recovery of their tissues. Lentils, soybeans, grains, and nuts were cheaper and popular alternatives when vegetable curries needed a meaty complement for those who were already grown and healthy.

When it could be afforded, fish was the most widely consumed source of animal protein in the village. Depānama, though not a coastal village, was still close enough to the coast that fish caught and hauled onto shore at dawn could reach our table for lunch the same day, but only because of Peethara, the fishmonger of Depānama.

Early in the morning, the fresh catch was brought into the bustling fish market at Borella in large ice-filled cartons and distributed to fish stalls in outlying towns. Peethara got on his bicycle and started his journey to the fish stalls, just as the first cartons were unloaded off the fishing boats and onto trucks bound for the market. He must have started his journey well before sunrise. He reached his destination just as the first cartons were emptied onto large concrete slabs at the stalls, and from there he selected not more than a few pounds of fish. Peethara did not have a truck or a bullock cart to fill up. Instead, he had a box fixed onto the back of his bicycle with enough space for the few pounds of fish he selected. He packed the fish tightly and sprinkled ice shavings and sand to keep it cold until it could be sold on his morning rounds. Then he made his way back to Depānama.

Peethara the fishmonger sold fish from the wooden box attached to the rear end of his bicycle each morning along the Borella-Kottāwa Road in Depānama. I didn't know how he knew, but he always seemed to arrive at the right time. It was the time of morning when Āchchā and my Youngest Aunt sat in the armchairs on the veranda discussing the lunch menu. Peethara would come up the incline along the Borella-Kottāwa Road, travelling from the direction of Borella towards Kottāwa on his bicycle, crying out, "Fish! Fish!" Had he arrived a moment too late, the menu would already have been decided upon and they would have opted for having dried fish for lunch. Had he arrived a moment too soon, it would have been too early to purchase fish for lunch.

Peethara lived with his extended family in Polwatte, past Depānama towards Borella on the Borella-Kottāwa Road, by the side of the rice fields. His appearance, like his routine, did not change from day to day. He wore the same faded, tattered shirt and sarong every day. The grey and white stubble on his face never grew to the length of a full beard, but never looked like it had been shaven either. The length of his hair was almost the same as that of the stubble on his face, and both formed one continuous growth.

From her chair on the veranda, Āchchā called out to Peethara as his bicycle slowed down expectantly in front of the Elephant Gates.

He would stop his bicycle but not get down. With one foot resting on one of his pedals, and with the other on the ground, he would wait for Āchchā to come to him. He would snatch his hat off his head and pull his sarong down to cover his knees as a mark of courtesy. When Āchchā opened the Elephant Gates and let us out onto the side of the road, we crowded around his bicycle excitedly.

"Aah! Peethara?" Āchchā said by way of both inquiry and greeting.

"Our Lady?" replied Peethara, also by way of both inquiry and greeting.

These preliminaries done with, they then got down to business.

"So what have you got for us today?"

The lid of the box would be opened and Āchchā would examine its contents critically. Standing on tiptoe, we clamored beside her for a peek into his fish box, our curiosity exceeding our revulsion at the sight of dead fish. Reaching into his box, he brought out his prime specimens and held each up horizontally with both hands for display. His box was too small to hold large fish like seer, kingfish, tuna, or shark, so it was only the smaller varieties he carried. Sometimes all he had was small sardines, and on those days he let Āchchā know even before he opened the box so she could decide if she wanted to bother with an inspection.

Āchchā never haggled over prices with village tradesmen like my mother did. If Peethara quoted a price Āchchā thought to be too high, she became suddenly silent. She let him see the doubt in her eyes and the downward slope of her mouth indicating displeasure. Bargaining was a subtle and silent language when the ladies of the village spoke it, and although Peethara did not have the privilege of speaking it himself, he understood it well. If he persisted, Āchchā indicated that the transaction was over by the swish of her housecoat and a slight turning of her head in the direction of the house. Peethara had only a few hours before the ice over his fish melted and it started to spoil. It was critical that he make the sale. He conceded defeat with head bowed. The price was quickly lowered or a better value for Āchchā's money pointed out.

Once the choice of fish and its price had been settled upon, Peethara took out his cleaver, which he kept tucked safely between the handles of his bicycle and cutting board. It was a heavy and dangerous weapon and, as if to prove this point, it was always stained with blood. Peethara handled it expertly.

Delicately, he placed the selected fish flat on his wooden cutting board for Āchchā to take a closer look. Holding her hands behind her back, she bent over the fish. First, she made sure the fish was indeed the species that Peethara claimed it was. She looked into the eyes of the fish, knowing that fish eyes were transparent when fresh and turned opaque when decomposing. She scrutinized the scales and gills to make certain these structures were intact. Once Āchchā nodded that she was satisfied, Peethara wielded his cleaver with considerable dexterity, and in one swift motion cut off the head and then the tail of the fish. He did not throw these parts out, but put them back into his box to be sold for a cheaper price. Fish heads and tails were used for the making of fish-head curry. Making a side slit along the body, Peethara hooked the internal organs with his index finger and removed them. He flung the fish guts carelessly onto the side of the road, where a stray cat or dog would be sure to make a quick meal of it. Next he cut the fish into cubes. Amazingly, he then pulled out yet another apparatus. This time it was an old rusty beam balance. He placed the fish cubes on one plate and loaded either a quarter-, half-, or one-pound iron weight on the other, depending upon the weight of fish Āchchā was buying. He held the balance up high and waited for the needle to settle. Once Āchchā nodded agreement, he emptied the fish onto a piece of soggy, bloodstained newspaper, wrapped it, and handed it to my Youngest Aunt. Āchchā paid him in cash and completed the transaction.

At Kshānti, lunch was served at noon on the big dining table in the dining room at the back of the house. Red rice was the staple and the main dish. The rice consumed at Kshānti was from Āchchā's own fields. Each morning, her cook boiled a large cauldron of rice in the kitchen at Kshānti. It filled the house with a warm, nutty, starchy aroma. Enough was boiled not just for the midday meal, but also for the evening meal and afternoon snack. Enough was boiled not just to feed the household, but also occasional visitors and those running errands and bringing messages to the house. Once the table was laid for lunch, the dishes were only cleared just before dinner. It was the custom, in those days, to offer a meal of rice and curry to anyone entering the house. No one was allowed to leave hungry. Two or three side dishes of vegetables were cooked to go with the rice. A finely chopped salad of green leaves mixed with onions, scraped coconuts, and limejuice made it to the table regularly and went well with red rice. Potatoes, eggplant, okra, pumpkin, green beans, gourds, and cucumber were all Āchchā's favorites. Both my Youngest Aunt and Āchchā liked to cook fish in chili-flavored water without the addition of coconut milk. With this method of preparation, the cooked fish lasted several hours without spoiling.

My Youngest Aunt was sometimes suspicious of the quality of the purchases they made from Peethara. Before eating his fish, she broke up the pieces with her fingers and tasted. "Mother," she said looking troubled, hesitating before serving my young cousins, her children, "Do you think Peethara may have cheated us?"

"Nonsense!" said Āchchā, defending Peethara. "Peethara will not cheat me. It is the cooking that is at fault," laying the blame squarely on the cook.

Competitively priced, locally made refrigerators started to make their way into the Depānama kitchens, and storage became less of a problem. My Uncle Dhaham replaced the small fridge in the dining room with a larger one with a separate freezer compartment. On Saturdays my parents, aunts, and uncles shopped at the commercial fish markets in Colombo and brought home large cuts of tuna, seer, and kingfish. At Kshānti, my Youngest Aunt portioned out the amount needed for each day and froze the fish in separate packages in her new freezer.

When Peethara slowed down at the Elephant Gates, hoping to hear his name called, neither my Youngest Aunt nor Āchchā stopped him to inquire after what he had in his box. If he stopped, they let him know that they had enough fish in the home to last for several weeks. A well-stocked fish stall opened up at the Pannipitiya Junction and those in Depānama who went up to Pannipitiya on errands stopped by there.

Peethara's consumers had moved on to new and improved marketing practices. The morning trek and the anxious search to make a deal were wearing out Peethara. There must have been a day when he didn't awaken before dawn and get up on his bicycle for the trip to get his fish box filled. He probably didn't know that it would be the day when Depānama lost its last fishmonger.

13

Offerings

Flowers were essential assets for Āchchā. She offered them to the Buddha each morning and evening. A small podium had been constructed on the wall in the front room at Kshānti and a white clay statue of the Buddha placed on it. My Uncle Dhaham had made the podium by mounting a broad, flat piece of wood on the wall with metal mounting brackets. It stood at a level a little higher than our heads, as was suitable for the offering of flowers to the Buddha. On full moon days, Āchchā went to the temple. She also went on pilgrimages to the ancient citadels and holy sites in the North and in the South. She had been on two pilgrimages to India, paying homage at places connected to the life of the Buddha, but she needed to practice her devotion on a daily basis, and the Buddha statue mounted on the wall in the front room helped her do just this.

Flowers were an instrument of homage, a symbolic offering expressing obeisance, reverence, and faith. They were placed at the foot of the Buddha statue, around the *stupa* mound, and at the root of the *bo-fig* tree in the temple. Spirituality was a way of life and an exercise needing daily reinforcement. Just as Āchchā did in the front room at Kshānti, many homes in Depānama had a high place—a podium, the top of a cupboard, or a cabinet top—dedicated to the offering of flowers to the Buddha. Men, women, and children made salutations and recited stanzas at the start and end of the day. They hoped these actions would bless them with mild weather, a better harvest, freedom from illness, good fortune, and success. Āchchā did not want these things. Her duties in this life were done. Her wishes and goals were now for fulfillment in the next life. Though she had never expressed her thoughts directly to me, I knew she yearned to meet her husband again in another life. I knew this was something that he too would have wished for before his passing.

Oddly enough, flowers were not offered to the living. It was not the custom in those days to take bouquets of flowers when visiting sick relatives. When visiting sick relatives, it was more useful to take them dishes of cooked curries, fruit, soothing oils, and applications. The men in the village did not woo the women with bouquets of flowers either. It was usual to take offerings of rice, sweets, fruits, curd, and treacle to the woman's parents, inform them of matrimonial intentions, and proceed from there in a roundabout way. When a prospective bride was approached by a groom, it was much more practical to offer her a home and bountiful crops than waste time on such frivolities. At least that was the thinking in those days.

Āchchā did not pick every kind of flower for her offerings, for not all flowers were suitable. White flowers were preferred for the purity and serenity the color represented. White did not evoke desire, but rather repelled it. The flowers that Āchchā picked for her offerings smelled only faintly sweet. Heady pungent perfumes only excited the senses. They did not induce tranquility.

The *sepalika* tree stood at the side of the house, outside the window of my Youngest Aunt's and Uncle Dhaham's room. *Sepalika* is a night blooming jasmine. It was different from most other trees I had seen, for it had no trunk, but branches that seemed to have sprung from the ground itself. Each individual branch was as tall as Āchchā's house. My brother and I had tried to climb it many times, but the tall slender branches stood straight and their smooth surface offered us no foothold. The sandpaper-like coarseness of its dark green leaves was not pleasant when it rubbed against our arms and legs. The *sepalika* was a favorite with Āchchā, and I think she was secretly relieved that the tree was able to protect itself from our intrusions.

Āchchā visited the *sepalika* each morning. The tree bore its flowers on the tips of its high branches. The flowers opened in the early hours of the morning and the tree shed them at sunrise, while the morning dew still lay on the ground to refresh the fallen blooms. The flowers were small and delicate, with five white petals attached to a bright orange stalk. They had to be picked from the ground with care, for the tender petals bruised easily and browned. Bending over, Āchchā would pick each one up by the stem and drop them into my hands as I held them out for her. We picked only a handful of flowers, the rest we left where they had fallen. "They are for the ants and the fruit flies," said Āchchā. The flowers were sprinkled with water and arranged in a semicircle on a small white saucer before being placed in front of the Buddha.

The *bamba* trees had been so named by my young cousin, the youngest son of my Youngest Aunt, for its small round fruit. The fruit was inedible but a favorite of his to pick and play with. He would break apart the outer shell and examine its numerous seeds with care. Though each *bamba* fruit looked the same to me, it seemed that he found something to captivate him in each one he broke apart. This cousin was younger than me by several years, and if I had a cousin who could be called cute and cuddly, it was he. As a young child, he had a "live and let live" carefree philosophy that we, his older cousins, adored. We played with him whenever he consented to play with us. We watched my Youngest

Aunt bath him in his blue plastic basin, dress him in rompers, feed him his favorite meal of rice mixed with butter and fish, and rock him to sleep in her arms. We watched his little rounded body lying curled up on my aunt's bed as he slept. Most of all we liked to hug him. We liked to fold him in a close and tight embrace until breathless, impatient, and uncomfortable, he wriggled his chubby limbs free and ran away laughing and giggling.

Both Āchchā and my Youngest Aunt loved the flowers of the *bamba* tree. Two *bamba* trees grew opposite each other, one at each of the posts of the Elephant Gates. The trees were tall with slender, pliable branches that bent easily and yielded both its plentiful flowers and fruit. The flowers themselves were naturally imperfect. The rounded white petals that opened from the thin long stalks were crinkled and uneven, each flower unique and different from the other. They were not as delicate as the *sepalika* and didn't bruise when my young cousin groped with his pudgy fingers to pluck them. Unlike the *sepalika*, which bloomed unseen, the *bamba* was not secretive. It bloomed in bright daylight.

To make offerings were a part of life not only in health but also in sickness. When incurable states of illness such as cancers and strokes afflicted elderly relatives, causing pain, debility, and death, and no cure could be found even at the General Hospital in Colombo, villagers struggled to understand why. They suspected their neighbors and enemies of casting evil spells or secretly administering sickening potions. When perfectly hale and hearty youth manifested strange behavior, they attributed it to being possessed by demonic influences. When diseases such as measles, mumps, and chicken pox periodically spread in young children, like ripples in a pond starting from a single case, they held heavenly deities responsible. In the village it was easier to place blame on the unknown and unseen than to seek an explanation through science. When naturally occurring climatic cycles brought drought, heavy rains, turbulent winds, or pest invasions to the village, the villagers didn't look for answers in a deeper understanding of the forces of nature, but attributed these disasters to the powerful impact of angry spirits.

At these confusing and desperate times, an emissary from the spirit world in human form was needed in the village. A liaison was required between this world and that, to bring good luck and better fortunes back. Depānama had a man who did just that. He was the *kapurala. Kapurala* was not a name given to any one person at birth, but the acquired title of an intergalactic liaison. It was not that the *kapurala* chose his profession but that the profession chose him, based on special characteristics exhibited at birth and a propensity to go in and out of trances and recite verses in a multitude of ancient languages. No one knew what his real name was. No one dared to ask. To heighten the sense of mystery surrounding him, he accentuated his white sarong and shirt with a fiery red scarf draped around his neck representing the color of blood.

When his services were needed, a message was sent and he would arrive for a preliminary consultation to obtain a history of the calamity and make a recommendation as to what manner of ritual ceremony was required to turn things around. He gave the household a list of offerings to be made ready for the appointed day. For these rituals, flowers were gathered in colors of red, purple, blue, orange, and bright yellow. Deities of other worlds craved the pleasure of sight and bright floral offerings satisfied these desires in them. Heavy pungent scents such as gardenia and jasmine satisfied their need for pleasurable aromas, and these were also offered. The *kapurala* also requested incense sticks, clay oil lamps, strips of cotton in blue, red, and yellow, and in some cases a supply of lime fruits.

Usually a temporary sitting area was arranged using floor mats, either indoors or outdoors, depending on how public the ceremony. Some households kept these proceedings quiet, while others made a social occasion of them, inviting neighbors and relatives and serving snacks and refreshments. A podium was constructed by placing boxes or planks at a higher elevation than the sitting area and draping them in white cloths. On it were placed offerings of flowers, incense sticks, and clay oil lamps, according to the *kapurala*'s specifications. At the start of the ritual, surrounded by the interested parties and their well-wishers, the *kapurala* began his rhythmic recitations in ancient languages, motioning with his arms and sometimes rocking his body to and fro with his eyes closed. At intervals, he lit the lamps and waved the incense sticks. He took the strips of brightly colored cloth and tied them around the affected person's torso. He threw flowers in the air and sprinkled water around. In cases where the "evil eye" was suspected, he made an elaborate show of cutting up limes and dropping them into a pail of water, symbolically cutting out the effect of the evil eye. When he finally made the connection with the other world, he went into a trance-like state and made rapid, unintelligible utterances. He would later explain that he had been making the case on behalf of his worldly clients to underworld powers. Highly paid *kapuralas* of the day came with their own dance troops, drummers, and horn-blowers. They wore colorful masks and traditional costumes and danced to the beat of drums and horns. The ceremonies they conducted went on until the early hours of the morning.

A miraculous turning of the tides was expected and frequently said to occur after the efforts of the *kapurala*, but there was no loss of confidence if it didn't. People moved on and what, by one means or the other, couldn't be changed was blamed on fate.

14

The Bucket

EVERYONE IN THE VILLAGE HAD A ROLE to play: an administrative, economic, social, or cultural niche to fill and function within. The wealth in the village was held by the landowners. There were only a handful of families in the village with this distinction at the time, and those born into these families were born into a role of affluence and influence. The administrators and entrepreneurs earned a steady and reasonable income and led comfortable lives. They enjoyed the respectability that came with their responsibilities. Some roles, such as rice farming, were a way of life passed down from generation to generation. Others in the village found their calling upon discovery within themselves of a specialized talent such as cookery, embroidery, carpentry, or masonry. They perfected their skills throughout their lives and their services were sought after in the village. Some were neither talented nor wealthy, but good with pen and paper. They found work as shop assistants, peons, and bookkeepers. Unskilled casual labor, fieldwork, and construction were popular among both men and women as a means of earning a livelihood when all else failed and there were still mouths to feed at home. Some were skilled at labor, such as coconut plucking, *chena* cultivation, rubber tapping, and buffalo herding. Any kind of labor was still hard work and did not provide for more than a hand-to-mouth existence, with little allowance for luxuries or comforts.

Even though each in the village, by one means or another, eventually found their calling and settled into their stations and roles, Piyasena was one who had failed to do so. No one knew when or where he was born or how he got to Depānama. It seemed he had entered directly into adulthood, found himself in the village, and looked around dazed and bewildered not knowing how he was going to sustain himself or find shelter from the elements. It may have been this perpetual daze in Piyasena that led those who encountered him to wonder if all his faculties were intact or if he had taken leave of some of them. Those in the village more fortunate than him took to him kindly and handed down to him their used clothes. If he was seen to be loitering around at meal times, he was handed a plate of rice and curry. He was allowed shelter on an open veranda on a rainy night. This did not mean that he received luncheon invitations or that those in the village opened up their homes to him, for they didn't. Such invitations would only have hurt his reputation, built upon unpredictability and bizarre behavior.

Eventually, many in the village supposed that Piyasena was simply mad. Then one full moon day, a day when emotional instability was said to be accentuated, this widely held suspicion was confirmed. The police apprehended Piyasena after he stole a dozen steel buckets from a hardware store in Colombo. He was said to have confessed to his crime without hesitation. It was obvious that he had committed it, but when the police asked him why he had done so and what he wanted a dozen steel buckets for, he had no explanation. The police confiscated the buckets but let him go. He was not a criminal, they concluded, but simply a madman affected by the full moon. The story spread in the village, and Piyasena acquired the notoriety that guaranteed him his means of existence. His name was forgotten after this incident. He became known simply as the "Bucket." He perfected his role by exaggerating his every idiosyncrasy and eccentricity, leaving no doubt in those who encountered him that he was indeed mad.

Though Piyasena had serendipitously happened upon this role that suited him so well, it was by no means his own invention. In an earlier era when my mother and aunts were children, the role of the madman of the village was taken by a character much more flamboyant than the Bucket. He was known as the "Coconut Shell Lunatic" for his signature habit of wearing a garland of coconut shells around his neck. My mother and aunts, who confessed without shame that his appearance at the Elephant Gates usually caused them to seek safety beneath their beds, feared him. They described him as wild and violent, and I was glad that he had passed away before I was born and that all we had to contend with in Depānama now was the Bucket. As I grew up, I realized that instead of being more fearful or wild, the Coconut Shell Lunatic may have just been more invested in his role.

The Bucket must have lived somewhere in the village, but I did not know where. If he lived in any one place at all, it can't have been more than a singleroom abode of clay and thatched coconut leaves, perhaps by the side of the rice fields. He had no need for necessities other than the food and clothing for which he relied on the generosity of others. He would have no need for a dresser, a cabinet, or a cupboard for his pots and pans. The only light he probably needed was the light of the sun in the daytime and the light of the moon in the night. He must have slept on a reed mat on the floor. He had no known relatives. At least there were none in the village who claimed any kinship to him. If he knew of anyone who was related to him, the Bucket kept quiet about it.

If he bathed, he gave no indication of it. If he washed or changed his clothes, he gave no indication of this either. Yet, rather than convey an appearance of gradual deterioration, he conveyed one of purposeful neglect. His sarong was dirty and torn. His shirt must have been white at one time, but was now streaked with brown dust. His clothes hung about his frame loosely. A mane of shaggy pepper-gray hair fell over his forehead. The uneven stubble on his face hinted at having been trimmed with a knife rather than shaved with a blade. He strived to express disdain for decorum by hoisting his sarong up well over his knees and leaving his shirt open over his chest. His step was jaunty when he walked, as was the swing of his arms.

Sometimes in the mornings and sometimes in the late afternoons, the Bucket made his way along the Borella-Kottāwa Road in front of Kshānti. Though his routine was predictably unpredictable, he never failed to look out for Āchchā, peering at the veranda from the roadside, hoping to see her at her place in the armchair. The Bucket liked to come in and sit on the veranda steps when he spotted Āchchā there. This meant that she was relaxing, free from her chores. At the sight of Āchchā in her familiar place, a smile of pleasure would spread across his face. Pulling his sarong down hastily to cover his legs, he would rattle the Elephant Gates, calling out to Āchchā, "Our Lady!" before entering and approaching. "Ah! Piyasena!" Āchchā nodded and acknowledged the Bucket when he took his usual seat on the front step. He was careful to fold his legs neatly over the step below. He kept his head bowed and waited for Āchchā to prompt him into speech. "So, Piyasena?" was the only cue he needed from her to launch into a monologue of news, views, and escapades in and about the village. Save an occasional "Humph!" or "Ah!" Āchchā rarely tried to converse with him, but she listened to him without expressing judgment. She did not laugh at him openly or mock him secretly, as most in the village did. Āchchā had known the Bucket from the time she came to Depānama. He had a familiarity with the household at Kshānti that permitted this manner of regular impromptu visits.

There were days when the Bucket acted his part and his company on the veranda was best avoided. Word travelled up and down the Borella-Kottāwa Road that he was acting up. On those days, Āchchā kept an eye out for him, and when he squinted into the veranda looking for her, she silently stepped into the front room before being seen. There was no need to padlock the gates and lock the doors. An empty veranda was all that was needed to deter him from coming in, even in his maddest moments.

If the Bucket had failed to appear at the Elephant Gates for a week or so, it caused Āchchā and my Youngest Aunt to inquire of each other, "What do you suppose is wrong with the Bucket?" But sooner or later news of his antics would come in, reassuring us that he was alive, well, and thriving. He had a reputation for making a commotion at the Junction of the Four Mango Trees or the Pannipitiya Junction. These were public venues suited for the display of emotional outbursts and tirades. I had seen him myself on occasion gesturing wildly, holding the hem of his sarong even higher than usual. There were general topics that set him off, like political corruption, the decline of religious values, and soaring grain prices. He shouted out his opinions and held speeches along the roadside. Those in the village who knew him, and most did, stopped momentarily and moved on. Those who did not stared curiously. The topics of his tirades, however, rarely offended anyone in particular. He made neither personal attacks nor references.

The only thing that truly infuriated the Bucket was to be called the Bucket in public. His reaction upon being addressed this way was instantaneous, violent, and dramatic. Most in the village had witnessed this reaction and were careful not to call him the Bucket within his earshot, but the younger generation lacked these sensibilities and resorted to shouting out his acquired name as he passed by. His rage ignited, he would give chase, hurling obscenities with his tongue and sticks and stones with his hands. The Bucket rarely caught up with his tormentors, and his missiles rarely hit their mark. Panting and beaten, he would then resort to calling out threats of bodily injury and death to all those who insulted him.

When she heard about these incidents, Āchchā, in her armchair, brought up the subject delicately the next time she saw the Bucket: "I heard there was some trouble at the junction, Piyasena." Ashamed and full of regret, he sought to downplay the report: "They wouldn't leave me alone and I got a little angry." He gave his side of the story and Āchchā listened. We worried he might get picked up by the police for his outbursts, but the nearest police station was at Maharagama, several miles away, with bigger fish to fry than a case of disturbance of the peace by the Bucket. Āchchā cautioned him gently when it was his turn to listen.

When Āchchā felt the visit was at an end, she issued Piyasena the invitation he eagerly expected and always humbly accepted: "Go to the back and have a cup of tea. Have some food before you go." "Great merit to you, Our Lady!" He bowed his head and thanked her. He went around to the back of the house and had his meal sitting on the kitchen step. He sipped his cup of plain tea slowly with a piece of sweet *jaggery*. When he left, he left quietly. When he reached the roadside, he adjusted his shirt and hoisted up his sarong to its previous state of exposure and assumed the swagger in keeping with the Bucket of Depānama.

15

Pension Day

On the morning of the pension day, Āchchā awoke at her usual time. Whatever Āchchā did, she preferred to avoid the morning crowd. Āchchā got ready to go when my Uncle Dhaham had gone off to work and my younger cousins, the children of my Youngest Aunt, had gone off to school and the noise of the occasional traffic along the Borella-Kottāwa Road had subsided.

She was a trained teacher and had earned her living as such even before she met my grandfather. She continued in her profession until her retirement. When she retired, she started to receive a monthly payment from the government for her past service. The money arrived in cash to the post office at the Pannipitiya Junction. Upon presentation of the national identity card to the clerk, the pensioner was paid his or her pension in cash. Pension day was as regular and as inevitable in its occurrence in a monthly cycle as was the full moon day. Although Āchchā knew perfectly well when the pension day was, she still took pleasure in marking it down on her calendar.

Pension day was a special day for sure, but not so special that Āchchā wore her sari in the *Kandyan* style, as she did on formal occasions. This trip to the Pannipitiya Junction was not a social one, but rather one of practical necessity, and when practicality was called for, she wore her sari in the Indian style. For these long walks, Āchchā purposely wore the sari short, not letting it fall any longer than the ankles, to keep its hem free of mud and dust. If it took her fancy, she would wear a bead necklace, but no gold. The time and place for gold adornments were weddings and formal family gatherings. The post office was neither the time nor place for jewelry. Āchchā took with her such practical necessities as her purse, with enough change for the bus should she need to take the bus, and her umbrella. For walking, she wore her most comfortable leather slippers.

Āchchā had always walked to the post office, a distance of about two miles from Kshānti. On her way to the post office she passed through the Junction of the Four Mango Trees, past the home of my Middle Aunt, and past our own home, both on the left. She then crossed the railway line and turned to the right to arrive at the post office. For years, my mother had tried to put a stop to these visits. My mother argued that a long walk to collect her pension at the post office was beneath the dignity of a lady such as Āchchā, the widow of the village headman and the mother of his daughters, especially the eldest.

"You have no need for this minuscule pension," she said.

"My pension helps me," said Āchchā.

"I will give you what you need," she said.

"It will be an unnecessary burden for you," said Āchchā.

"The post office is too far," she said.

"I am used to walking," said Āchchā.

"I will go in the car and collect it for you," she said.

"I do not wish to trouble you," said Āchchā.

My Youngest Aunt approached the problem in a different way. On pension day she worried about Āchchā's trip to the post office from the moment she awoke, even before her husband and children left the house.

My Youngest Aunt often stood at the door of Āchchā's room watching her mother as she dressed. She must have done this even as a child.

"It is too hot today," she said.

"What if it is even hotter tomorrow?" said Āchchā.

"What if a purse snatcher snatches your purse?" she said.

"It will be safe tucked under my arm," said Āchchā.

"There were sightings of a rabid dog on the road this morning," she said.

"I have this umbrella to beat it with," said Āchchā.

"There have been reports of a jewelry thief in Depānama lately," she said.

"This umbrella works well for jewelry thief and rabid dog alike," said Āchchā.

When Āchchā emerged silently victorious, my Youngest Aunt changed her strategy and joined her. They stood side by side on the veranda and scrutinized the weather together.

"Take note of that cloud, Mother," my Youngest Aunt advised.

"Certainly I will," agreed Āchchā, "it looks heavy with rain."

They peered up and down the road together.

"Take care of the buses and the cars, Mother. If it was just the bullock carts it wouldn't be so bad," my Youngest Aunt cautioned.

"Without doubt," agreed Āchchā.

She checked that her purse was securely fastened and, as promised, tucked it under her arm. Her final act was to open her umbrella. If it wasn't raining, it was sunny, and a good umbrella worked for both sun and rain, among other things. Mother and daughter said goodbye to each other at the Elephant Gates. My Youngest Aunt watched Āchchā as she strolled leisurely, until she disappeared from sight around the bend.

The Borella-Kottāwa Road made a sharp turn at the Pannipitiya Junction to the left towards the town of Kottāwa. It also made a sharp turn to the right towards Maharagama. The post office stood at the start of the rightward turn.

The post office itself must have been the ancestral house of some family at some point. It was built well back from the road with a long winding gravel driveway and had the construction that was classic for old homes of the time, with a veranda, ornately carved doors, and narrow inset windows. Like most old homes, it looked forlorn and neglected. It had a pair of wrought iron gates at the entrance where a tall bright red postbox stood. This was the only indication that the postal service operated within. None of the establishments at the Pannipitiya Junction, whether of state or private enterprise, had signs announcing their business. This was a time when everyone knew everyone else's business by repute alone, and there was no need to advertise it further by the erection of signs and banners.

The post office shed the look of abandonment on pension day. From the early hours of the morning to midday, there would form a long orderly line of patient pensioners all the way to the front gates. Āchchā stood somewhere along this line. Like her, all the ladies wore saris and carried umbrellas, so much so that sometimes the line appeared to consist entirely of opened and raised umbrellas. Āchchā probably knew most of those standing in line with her, for they had all served the government in one capacity or another. All were her peers and residents of Depānama, and most were related to her through her husband in one way or another. Though I had never stood in the pension line with her, I knew that Āchchā on these occasions must have permitted herself to gossip. These were her cronies, after all.

Once the pension was collected and the pension line exited, the company was not as exclusive, and Āchchā was not inclined to chat idly at the Pannipitiya Junction. A nod, a smile, or a brief exchange on the weather was all she permitted herself in public places. Parked under the ancient *bo-fig* tree, just in front of the post office and next to the railway station, were the taxis. These were known as "hiring cars" in those days and there were three of them. The drivers of the hiring cars knew Āchchā well. They had been hired by the family at Kshānti for trips to Colombo from the time Āchchā first arrived in the village, to the time her older daughters attended the University, to the time when she took her sick and ailing husband to the General Hospital. She must have stopped a little longer here.

The only bakery in Depānama was located in the heart of the Pannipitiya Junction and it was from here that bread was distributed twice a day to all of Depānama and most of Pannipitiya. Having collected her pension, Āchchā would stop by the bakery to pick up something to bring home to us, usually in a brown paper bag. Pension day was a treat for Āchchā and she wanted to make it a treat for us too.

Āchchā's return home was heralded by the clink of the Elephant Gates being opened from the outside. This was a familiar sound at Kshānti that could be heard through the house and all the way to the kitchen at the back. We were all relieved to see Āchchā when she returned home from one of these trips, but none as relieved as Āchchā herself. Closing and folding her umbrella as she stepped onto the veranda, she would head straight for an armchair. By the time she returned, it would be almost lunchtime and the sun almost at its peak. Her cotton jacket would be moist with large round stains of sweat, and her face flushed with the heat. Distracted by the brown paper bag we had come to expect upon Āchchā's return home, we barely noticed her distress. She would reach for the tall glass of water my Youngest Aunt had ready for her with one hand and hand over her the bag with the other. The oil stains on its outside indicated good things on the inside.

Āchchā got us *spunchie* from the bakery most of the time. *Spunchie* were cupcakes made with what must have been a sponge cake recipe at one time, but which had been given the Pannipitiya touch by using less eggs and margarine and more flour. Āchchā kept strict count of who was at home and did not bring more than one for each family member. No more and no less. Dipping her hand into the bag, my Youngest Aunt would bring out the *spunchie* one by one and hand it around, counting as she did so, to make sure Āchchā had purchased just the right number.

It was not always easy to get fresh *spunchie*, even though the bakery always assured Āchchā that they sold her only the best. Āchchā had been fooled once. "Mother, you have been sold moldy *spunchie*," my Youngest Aunt had exclaimed, holding one up with a fluffy grey white growth on top. Āchchā was surprised and embarrassed—surprised that she had been cheated and embarrassed that she had not discovered it for herself before she made the purchase. "It is dark inside the shop," she said. "The mold may not have been visible." I knew this to be true, for even though the bakery at the Pannipitiya Junction gave out an inviting aroma of warm bread, its interior was a chasm of darkness. It was lighted by nothing more than a single kerosene oil lamp. Āchchā was careful after this debacle. If the *spunchie* looked at all old, she brought home a loaf of butter cake, which my Youngest Aunt portioned out equally for everyone, leaving out no one.

As time passed, Āchchā started taking the bus home from the post office. Having stood in line at the post office for so long, we were relieved when she arrived home by bus. The bus service was frequent and the fare well under a rupee. Later, she started waiting at the Elephant Gates to take the bus to the post office in the morning as well. I did not know that she had started to get heart pains when she walked and that she found walking fatiguing. She still marked her calendar for pension day, for the pension still helped her, but eventually she started sending someone to collect it instead. Her umbrella lay folded upon her table next to her purse. She did not carry her purse under her arm as she used to, but still used it to keep her change.

My Uncle Dhaham bought sugar, flour, eggs, and margarine from Maharagama and my Youngest Aunt started to make cakes at home. The cakes she made were warm and moist when they came out of the oven and tasted much fresher than the ones from the bakery at the Pannipitiya Junction. She added raisins and dried melon to the batter, so they were fruity too. But even her best recipe couldn't capture the dense sweetness of the *spunchie*. It may have been that the essence of the *spunchie* was not in the flour, sugar, or eggs used in its making, but was acquired on the trip home with Āchchā, on pension day.

16

The Village Elephant

THE SOUND WAS UNMISTAKABLE and it caused a great deal of excitement. It was the sound of steel chains clanging and dragging on the tarred road in slow and steady rhythm. It caused excitement for my brother and me because it was the sound of the village elephant making its way down the Borella-Kottāwa Road.

The ownership of an elephant was a matter of wealth and prestige. Depānama had one man of such wealth and prestige. We had never seen him, but thought he lived down Araliya Gardens. Each evening, just around dusk, the elephant, led by its keeper, the mahout, made its way down the Borella-Kottāwa Road. Passing our home and the home of my Middle Aunt, it ambled through the Junction of the Four Mango Trees, went another mile or so down the road, passed Kshānti, and turned into Araliya Gardens to the home of its owner to rest for the night. This elephant had no tusks. It was of medium size as pachyderms go. It didn't toss its head arrogantly or swing its trunk carelessly. Instead it walked sedately by the side of its mahout, leaving plenty of room for traffic and pedestrians, and other users of the road. Its back legs were chained together at the ankles, allowing it to walk, but not to run or charge. It was the sound of these chains clanging and dragging on the tar road that we had come to associate unmistakably with the elephant. It was the somber sound of the king of the jungle forced to live and work among us, tamed and subdued, going home to its human master. We became used to seeing it and failed eventually to see it as anything other than docile and gentle.

A mahout is the caregiver and protector of a domesticated elephant. He trains it for its life in captivity. He is nothing without his elephant and the elephant is wild and lost among humans without its mahout. The elephant first meets its keeper upon being captured from the wild or upon its birth, if born in captivity. The bond that is formed if the two are compatible is said to stay with each for life.

Our mahout bore a resemblance to the Tree Trimmer, Coconut Plucker, and Buffalo Herdsman. He was lean and slightly built, with parchment-brown skin tanned by spending long hours in the sun. He wore his sarong at the waist and hoisted it up, leaving his thighs bare. He walked barefoot. This was not an appearance uncommon to those who earned a living by manual labor in the village, but the mahout had an indisposition to brag, boast, gossip, and hang out with the local crowd. He did not patronize the neighborhood tavern at the end of the day. The end of the day still found him with his elephant. For a human to place his life in the trust of a wild beast, and for that wild beast in turn to depend upon the human for its well-being and protection, contradicted the natural order of things. The seriousness of this predicament impacted every aspect of a mahout's life. Many in the village looked upon him as one answering a divine call.

As a mother keeps a cane to discipline the child she loves for its own good, the mahout carries with him a *henduwa*. This was a long and heavy pole with a steel or brass hook at its end. It appeared very much like an ancient instrument of torture. I am sure to an elephant it must have appeared especially so. When an elephant became unruly, the mahout hooked its ear with the *henduwa* to bring it to order. Whether he used it or not, it was the mark of the mahout to carry a *henduwa*, just as it was the mark of a tree trimmer to carry a machete, the mark of a coconut plucker to carry a coir ring to hold his feet together when climbing coconut palms, and the mark of a buffalo herdsman to carry a stick to beat upon the backs of the buffalo to keep the herd together.

The elephant is a symbol of prosperity, loyalty, and protection, a creature of the gods. It was a symbol favored in the village above all other symbols. Its image was printed on draperies, linens, and clothing, and was carved onto jewelry and furnishings. Even Āchchā, who used no decorations or ornaments to lighten the utilitarian look of her living room at Kshānti, kept upon her coffee table the wooden figurines of two black elephants. They only added to the heavy feel of the room, but they had been present from the time her husband was alive and I knew they had special meaning to her, as did everything associated with his memory.

The appearance of an elephant along our road was neither strange nor unusual in those days. It was a common sight up and down the Borella-Kottāwa Road, especially at the start of *Perahara* season, when the great temples held their annual parades. The grandest annual parade of the island is the parade of the Kandy Temple in the central hill country of Kandy. Elephants from all over the island are invited to participate in this parade. They make their way on foot with their mahouts, travelling for many days to get to Kandy from their places of origin. If we did not always witness their journey, we still had evidence of it by the regularly spaced mounds of green fibrous dung left along the roads they traversed. The temple of popularity and repute closest to Depānama was the temple of Bellanvila, about twenty minutes' driving distance from Maharagama. This temple owned an imposing tusker who was frequently seen along the Borella-Kottāwa Road, attended by not one, but two, mahouts. But the elephant of Depānama is the one who had endeared itself to my brother and me. It knew nothing of our existence, and yet, as children often did, we felt we knew it well.

My father, having moved to the village only upon his marriage to my mother, had a natural curiosity about those who lived in it and often invited them into our home for a chat. My mother, having been raised in the village, had no such curiosity. She said she knew far more than she needed to know about those who lived in the village. My father, having arrived home early from work one day, watched at the gates with us. As usual, we heard it before we saw it. Regardless of how many times we had seen this elephant before, or indeed any other one before, the sight never ceased to fill us with wonder. They are magnificent and majestic to behold. My father must have been moved by this sight just as much as we were. As the elephant was passing our gates, my father called out to the mahout, "The leaves of our jack trees are young and plentiful. Your friend might enjoy them. It can pull down the branches with its trunk." The mahout signaled for the elephant to stop, smiled, and nodded. My father was typically impulsive and often acted upon his impulses without thought of consequence. But he, like we, knew when all was said and done, we still had our mother to answer to. We were filled with apprehension at what he had just done: What would our mother say?

We had more than fifteen big jack trees on a wide expanse of lawn. The trees were planted by my grandfather and were at least three times as tall as an elephant, with dense, lush branches spreading out three times as wide as one. I am sure both creatures, the two legged and the four legged, must have marveled at our jack trees as they passed by our house daily and wondered at how succulent the leaves must taste. The mahout guided his elephant through the gates and onto our lawn. This was the closest I had ever been to such a large and powerful animal. Every part of its body was fascinating just by itself. Its legs were stout and sturdy, and the skin folded over its joints as it moved. Dried mud was caked in the grooves between the wrinkles across its shoulders and back. There were sparse long hairs along the spine, only noticeable upon close inspection. It flapped its saucer-like ears slowly, and the blue veins coursing through them bulged prominently. It was a warm and humid afternoon, no different from any other. Standing underneath one of our trees and placing its front legs slightly apart, the elephant reached up with its trunk. Its tip was forked and came together like a giant thumb and index finger. Even without looking, it could feel out the youngest shoots and wrap the tip of its trunk around them. With one smooth motion, the young leaves were twisted off and delivered deep into the mouth of the elephant with its trunk. We could not see its molars from the outside, but could see the sideways grinding movement of its jaws. This was a vision my brother and I could only have daydreamed. When the animal started munching, the sound of vegetation being crushed and sheared was refreshing and satisfying. It must have been hungry. Even with its mouth still full, its trunk was reaching up and the sensitive tip feeling around for more. I found myself wondering what jack leaves tasted like. A strong odor of mud, foliage, dust, and dung had begun to permeate the surroundings. I inhaled deeply. I wanted to remember this earthy, organic smell more than any exquisite fragrance my father had brought home to my mother.

At some point, as I was watching the elephant, I became aware that the elephant was watching me. This was its natural vigilance and instinctive behavior, I knew. But having never been the subject of such vigilance before, I found it disconcerting, and I became aware of an instinct within myself telling me to move away. I moved closer to my father who was chatting with the mahout. "It is as curious of you as you are of him," he said. We found out that our elephant was a working elephant, pulling logs and felling trees at lumberyards and still a juvenile, not yet fully grown. My mother, too, joined us by the jack trees that day, but was uncharacteristically silent. It may have been that she too was affected by the grandeur of the spectacle, or it may have been that she also sensed the watchful eye of the creature upon her. When the elephant had had its fill and finally turned to leave, it made a wide circle, creating a whooshing sound, looking and sounding much like a ship in the port of Colombo. This vortex brought with it a fresh whiff of mud and dung right to our very nostrils. We were elated that we had had such a memorable visitor, yet relieved that the visit was over. My mother summed things up as usual. "The things," she said shaking her head, "your father will get up to."

When we first spotted the wound on the right flank of our elephant, we didn't think much of it. What harm could come to such a large creature from such a small wound, we thought. It must have had an accident at the lumberyard. But the wound became larger. It became so large that it had to be packed with cotton wool to keep the flies and maggots out. The careful, purposeful stride of our elephant became slow and pained. It held its head low and let its trunk hang limp when it walked.

After this, as suddenly as it had appeared one day before us, our elephant disappeared. It stopped its daily trek down our road and was never seen again. We didn't keep watch at the gates hoping to hear the familiar clink of iron chains. My brother and I did not talk about why our elephant had stopped coming. But there was hope in something Āchchā had told me once. "Life has no end," she said. "It is a wheel, turning again and again, man is reborn as beast and beast reborn as man. The elephant is a noble animal. It will be born again as a man, to live free and unafraid."

17

Checkers

Tea is a remarkable beverage. Every household in Depānama started the day with tea. The only type of tea served in the households of Depānama in those days was black tea. We knew of no other form or type of tea. Black tea is most aromatic and flavorful when brewed for at least ten minutes in freshly boiled water until inky red-brown. At Kshānti, tea was always served with milk and sugar, three times a day; first in the morning, as part of the breakfast, then at midmorning because lunch would still be at least two hours away. For the third time of the day, a jug of tea would be brewed in the midafternoon.

The heavy midday meal of rice and curry was like a sedative that took effect even before the meal was completed. At Kshānti, everyone headed for their afternoon naps right from the dining room. The only means of dispelling the hazy lethargy induced by the afternoon nap was the midafternoon cup of tea. This was, in my opinion, the most vital cup of tea. Āchchā and my Youngest Aunt would sit side by side in the armchairs on the veranda sipping their afternoon tea. We too would slump ourselves in the armchairs, flipping our slippers restlessly on the cement floor for the want of something to do. This was the time of day when the sun had started its downward journey but was still quite high in the sky. We were advised it was too hot to go outdoors. It was that lazy time of day when it was too much effort thinking about anything useful, far less actually doing anything useful. The Borella-Kottāwa Road was quiet. There were hardly any cars, buses, or bullock carts at this time of day. The evening rush hour was still several hours away.

My brother was not one to be content with peace and quiet. Trying to appear nonchalant, he would inquire carelessly, "Āchchā, shall we play checkers?" It sounded like a friendly invitation, but I knew differently. My brother was unpleasantly competitive. A game to him was not a game, but an opportunity to claim a victory. If at any time during a game he realized that this would be denied to him, he would create a dramatic scene and walk out. When he won, he celebrated by letting out whooping sounds and prancing about the room. He made sure everyone knew who had won and who had lost.

Despite these discouraging traits, my brother was frequently my only playmate. My cousins were not always available, and living so far from Colombo, we did not meet socially with our classmates. When we were stuck indoors on rainy days, we played cards, Ludo, and Snakes and Ladders. My brother enjoyed these games only when he was winning. When we returned from school, he and I played badminton, hopscotch, catchers, and rounders in our garden. When darkness fell, we were required to go in, wash up, and start our homework. These were my mother's rules. My brother refused to stop any game prematurely unless he was declared the victor, but when I was winning, he would be more than willing to call off a game on account of the darkness. We shared a bicycle that we rode up and down our driveway and around the lawn. When it was his turn, and it was his turn more than mine, he would zip around showing off.

This being the way things were between us, I was not particularly inclined to play checkers with my brother. It was one of his favorite games and one at which he could rarely be beaten, except perhaps by Āchchā. When my brother issued his supposedly friendly invitation, I supposed she too had seen the gleam in his eye and quick flare of his nostrils and known he was hungering for a win. That is where she and I differed: She accepted the challenge with pleasure.

The checkerboard was kept in the front room, which opened to the left of the veranda. The front room had no connection to the rest of the house and could only be entered from the veranda. It was the room in which my grandfather had conducted his duties as headman of Depānama. Āchchā did not like us going into the front room and disturbing its furnishings. In the center of the room stood my grandfather's writing desk with its thick wooden writing slab and two supporting columns of filing drawers, still smelling of old books and ink. The grain of the writing slab had acquired a purplish hue from the ink my grandfather had spilled on it over the years. Two large brown and white portraits, one of Āchchā and one of her husband, hung side by side on one wall. A row of five French windows opened out from the side of the room that faced the Borella-Kottāwa Road. In times past, villagers brought their disputes to this room, to the attention of my grandfather, to be mediated and settled. Sitting at his desk, he must have had a clear view through the long windows of those coming in through the Elephant Gates seeking his counsel. Each New Year my Uncle Dhaham whitewashed the walls of this room, as if to silence the voices of the turbulent time that was the history of Depānama.

Even though my brother had to stretch his arms as wide as he could to carry and support the checkerboard, he refused all help when fetching it. Two of the armchairs on the veranda were pulled to face each other. Āchchā sat on one and my brother sat on the other. The checkerboard was balanced precariously on the four ends of the arms of their chairs.

Checkers was a favorite game at Kshānti long before we were born. The smooth, well-worn surface of the checkerboard and pieces bore evidence of this. Like everything from the front room, the checkerboard smelled of ink.

The start of a checker game brought about an immediate sense of relief from the stupor of the afternoon. I usually perched myself on the arm of Āchchā's chair. My Youngest Aunt dragged her chair closer for a better view of the action. There were only four armchairs in the veranda, and my two young cousins, the children of my Youngest Aunt, usually squeezed into the last.

Setting up the checkerboard was serious business, and Āchchā and my brother assumed appropriately serious expressions during this task. Silently, deliberately, and carefully, each placed their twelve checker pieces in three rows of four, each starting from opposing ends of the board. This completed, each stared at the other's checker pieces, even before a single piece was drawn, like two wrestlers at the start of a fight measuring each other from opposing ends of the ring. Āchchā always let my brother choose first. She would let him choose which color checker pieces he wanted, white or black, and she gave him the choice of drawing the first checker piece. My brother always chose the white checker pieces because he believed white was lucky for him. He always let Āchchā draw first because he believed by doing this she would reveal her strategy early on.

These preliminary antics left us, the spectators, somewhat irritated. Not wanting to distract the players, my Youngest Aunt and I chose to express our impatience to each other by an exchange of furtive glances. So, it wasn't surprising when the drawing of the first checker piece brought an audible sigh of relief from all involved. The game was finally underway. Checker pieces, unlike chess pieces, were not picked up off the board when being moved, but rather pushed across the surface. The scraping sound would have been jarring at any other time but this, when all we were waiting for was the first move.

The first fifteen minutes of checkers was always the most exciting. Āchchā and my brother quickly moved their pieces in zigzag motions, bobbing and weaving into each other's half of the checkerboard, again, very much like two wrestlers who had now entered the center of the ring. They alternately trapped and jumped each other's checker pieces diagonally across the board, each moving his or her pieces gradually towards the center of the board.

My brother was loud and enthusiastic. He sat on the very edge of his chair and leaned forward. His movements were quick, and he expressed his thrills and frustrations decisively. Āchchā thought more, talked less, and relaxed. She leaned back in her chair between moves and allowed my brother plenty of time to make his. At least, this was how the game started out.

After this initial stage, when both sides had sustained quick gains and losses more or less equally, an invariable stalemate precipitated. The remaining checker pieces were precious to each player and neither was willing to make a move and give the other the advantage. They would both start to stare gloomily at the board. The player who was trapped and in imminent danger of losing a checker piece would lean forward and peer intently at the layout, contemplating the next move. The opponent, meanwhile, would lean back in an attitude of exaggerated boredom.

My Youngest Aunt and I would feel our initial impatience returning and would now break our silence and begin to offer helpful advice to try to break the stalemate. My Youngest Aunt, having two young boys of her own, felt it her duty to guide my brother to a win. As for my part, I was always on Āchchā's side. Checkers was not a strong point with my Youngest Aunt or me. We usually found that all the potential moves we suggested had not only been already considered by both players and rejected, but that they had also considered two to three subsequent moves and rejected these too. As helpers, we failed to help. Instead of breaking the stalemate, we broke the concentration of the participants. My brother would point out that instead of giving advice, I should take the challenge and play the game myself. Things were getting ugly for sure.

By this time, my Youngest Aunt and I joined forces by an exchange of looks. She had held me the very day I was born and was my closest friend and confidant from the time I could remember. We could read each other's subtlest expressions. There had never been a point in our lives when she and I had disagreed. She and I were now bored and disinterested in the outcome of the game. We didn't care who won or lost. We wanted to leave, but couldn't let the players down. They were, after all, family. While one spectator distracted the players, the other would attempt to surreptitiously move an outlying checker piece to tip the balance in favor of one player or the other. We didn't care who. Both players liked to keep the game clean and neither welcomed this intrusion. If caught, Āchchā would sternly admonish us both, and my brother would break out into an all-out fight with me. If things were ugly before, this was surely a battle zone around the checkerboard, and yet the stalemate continued.

If any of us on the veranda had bothered to look outside, we would have noticed the long shadows cast by the *plumeria* on the front of the house and the traffic starting to pick up on the Borella-Kottāwa Road, but we had no time for trivial observations in the heat of the checkers game. The strategy that ultimately brought an end to the game of checkers was decided upon by my young cousins, the sons of my Youngest Aunt, who had long since abandoned the veranda to play outside. They, tired of Āchchā's long preoccupation and wanting her back for themselves, would run in from outside, coated in dust and sweat, straight onto Āchchā's lap throwing their arms about her. They toppled the checkerboard and scattered the checker pieces across the veranda. "Hah!" my brother would shout, throwing up his arms in annoyance. "I was just about to win!"

18

The Water Buffalo

Āchchā's household awoke twice each day. The first was the early morning frenzy, when the sharp crunch of my Uncle Dhaham's rubber slippers could be heard through the house as he hurried to get ready for work. His lunch of rice and curries made that morning would be served on a plate, covered with another and tied with a large cotton napkin. He'd dash to his car, keys dangling, with brief case in one hand and his lunch in the other. Āchchā was still asleep, or if awake, kept to her room. Perhaps she thought it was best to keep out of his way.

The second awakening was one of my favorite parts of the day, and it was a dazed and gradual stirring from a deep midafternoon slumber. After lunch, both my Youngest Aunt and Āchchā retired to their rooms on either side of the living room. Very soon, the living room would fill with the drone of electric fans and soft snoring. Though we would rather not have wasted our time napping, the sweltering heat and humidity of midday made us drowsy and we too sought some space on Āchchā's bed or crept into the spare room for a nap.

This second awakening was gradual. Even before I opened my eyes, I would hear the sounds of the cars and buses on the road outside. The children of Depānama Junior School would shout and call to each other as they made their way home after school. I waited to hear the drag of feet along the cement floor, indicating that Āchchā was up. Then, I too would rise, immediately thirsty and hungry.

On these lazy warm afternoons, Āchchā instructed the making of snacks to go along with our tea. Depending on what ingredients were available, she decided on what was to be made. Sometimes we had *roti*, thick grilled flat bread made from flour and grated coconut. As a special touch, pieces of green chilies and onions were added to the dough. We ate these while still hot, tossing each from hand to hand to cool. Āchchā's favorite was *aggala*, round balls of toasted flour, sugar, and coconut. String hoppers are small stringy steamed cakes. When they are wrapped around a filling of coconut and caramelized sugar, they are called *lavariya*. If all we had were stale string hoppers, then these could be fried till crispy and drizzled with melted sugar. We had paper-thin oily crepes stuffed with coconut and melted sugar. *Halape* was a cake made from toasted flour, coconut, and sugar steamed between the folded halves of a *kanda* leaf. When done just right, the cake picked up the woody, leafy flavor of the *kanda*. We perched ourselves on the arms of the kitchen bench and watched and waited with dwindling patience until these were made. We were too young to wait for any food coming off the fire to cool down or even to make it to a plate.

I sat on the step at the back of the house beside Āchchā and my Youngest Aunt. Snacking between sips of their afternoon tea, revived and refreshed, they were already planning dinner. Together we watched the sun set in the distance, between the coconut palms behind the tamarind tree.

Sunset was a feeling rather than any specific time at Āchchā's place. We were tired and needing to go home. The garden had become a mass of shadows. Strange sounds and scurrying noises issued from familiar places. The house, too, was getting quiet. It seemed to me that the gathering darkness outside would shroud the house like it had done the garden. We had to gather our drawings, pictures, marbles, and other treasures to take home when our parents came to pick us up from Āchchā's place, where we had spent the day.

It was at this time that the herd of water buffalo made their way down Araliya Gardens, the gravel road running alongside Āchchā's property. The herd then turned onto the Borella-Kottāwa Road and made its way in front of Āchchā's house. The water buffalo worked in the rice fields that lay far behind Āchchā's house where Araliya Gardens tapered to an end. In the wet season they plowed the paddy fields and made them ready for the sowing of rice. In the dry season, when the sheaves were cut, they threshed the sheaves with their hooves to separate the grains from the hay. When not working, there was only one thing water buffalo liked to do. They liked to wallow in mud.

The brick wall that ran in front of the house separating it from the road was low and wide. At dusk, Āchchā, my Youngest Aunt, my two younger cousins, my brother, and I would gather here. We, the children, climbed onto and sat on the wall. My Youngest Aunt held my young cousins firmly by their waists once they got on the wall. She placed one arm around each of her children. We, being older, sat free from restraints, our bare feet dangling over the side.

The herd came up a slight incline as they approached the Elephant Gates. We both heard and smelled them before they came into view. An odor of dung and mud pervaded the air. The faint clip-clop of hooves grew louder. A few of the mature bulls wore jingles around their necks and the two sounds blended harmoniously as the first heads bobbed into view.

Water buffalo are stocky ruminants. Their legs are short and sturdy. Their shoulders are broad. The muscles on their flanks tense and protrude when they move. They have a habit of stretching their necks out low when they walk, making their heads nod up and down rhythmically. Though the potential for aggression is evident in the build of its body, its disposition is anything but aggressive. Water buffalo are even-tempered and mellow. Large eyes peering warily out from under heavy lids and lashes reveal this inner agreeable temperament. They unobtrusively sense the surroundings and taste the air with their large moist wrinkled muzzles.

The juveniles led the way. They held their heads high and their craned necks forward, sniffing the air with drippy, flaring nostrils. They jostled and pushed against each other, as they are prone to do at this stage of growth. We could see where several had started to grow horns. They instinctively set a leisurely pace for the rest of the herd. Some would come up on the grassy embankment to graze where we could almost touch the flecks of mud that had dried on their backs. The buffalo herdsman did not lead his charges and it was the young buffaloes with habitual practice that guided the herd to its home each evening.

There were a few mature males. They followed the juveniles nonchalantly. If the pace set by the juveniles was too slow, they moved ahead. If the pace was too fast, they didn't care to keep up and took their own time anyway. Oftentimes they nibbled by the roadside. They managed to convey an impression of boredom. I imagined they were bored of this daily trek, bored of the sights, sounds, and smells, and bored of the daily toil.

The calves were playful, curious, and full of energy. They were not used in fieldwork, and even at the end of the day still had plenty of pep left in them. They tried to do as the juveniles did. They sniffed the grass but could not stand still long enough to eat it. They had no control of their tails and threw them high up in the air haphazardly. They snorted needlessly and hit the ground hard with their hooves. For all this testing of the waters, they were still only calves and needed their mothers for protection and milk. The females travelled at the center of the pack and the calves were careful not to stray too far from them.

The road in those days was narrow, barely allowing two vehicles to pass. Most of the traffic down the road was on foot. Many in the village stopped to exchange a word with Āchchā and acknowledge her presence at the wall as we watched the buffalo. The herd took their time when they passed and owned the entire width of the road. An occasional car or bus avoided the buffalo by swerving off the road and onto the grassy embankment bordering it on either side. There were times when motorized traffic came to a halt altogether.

The older in the group were the stragglers who took up the end. They did not bother to keep up with the others. They swished their tails lazily at the mosquitoes and flies. Absentmindedly, they ground their jaws and chewed the cud. Occasionally a straggler would stop in the middle of the road and stare distractedly ahead as if forgetting where it was and what it was supposed to do. To break this trance and get the animal on its way, the buffalo herdsman would hit it on the rump with his stick. Sometimes this was not enough and he would combine the blow with an "Oopah!" sound delivered from deep within his throat. This usually did the trick.

The buffalo herdsman traveled with the stragglers. He made sure that none of his animals were left behind. He bore the marks of his labor, as did his herd. A line of mud on his calves demarcated how deep he had waded in the fields that day. He wore his sarong high on his thighs. His feet were bare as they slapped the tar. The mark of the buffalo herdsman was the stick. He selected his stick from the tall bushes of *watamara* that grew alongside the rice fields. The stem of this bush is long and straight without protruding branches. It is pliable enough to deliver a blow on the back of an animal and spring back into shape without breaking. The surface is even and comfortable to hold. As part of his morning routine, he spent a great deal of time selecting just the right stem and then trimming and polishing it until just the right length and smoothness had been achieved. When not prodding the stragglers to life from their weary daydreams, he carried his stick proudly on his shoulder like a spear.

The buffalo herdsman balanced an attitude of casual vigilance over his animals and remote disregard of all else. As if to demonstrate this point further, he cleaned his teeth with the brushy end of a twig as he strolled. He acknowledged no one and neither did his herd of water buffalo. He was one of our heroes, but he did not acknowledge us with a nod or a smile.

A few of the more prosperous farmers in Depānama bought tractors and rented them out to other farmers for use in the rice fields. The tractor symbolized the mechanization of rice growing in Depānama. The gigantic rear tires of a tractor when driven through the paddy parcels could plow and churn the mud quickly and methodically. Tractors were equally efficient at threshing paddy sheaves. What used to require a full day or more of labor by man and beast could be done in a matter of a single morning. Now it was the tractors that made their way down the Borella-Kottāwa Road at the end of the workday. Their huge rubber tires spewed mud all over the road as they moved noisily. When the water buffalo stopped coming, we did not worry on their account. The rich fatty buffalo milk was still coveted for its fermented curd. This was a delicacy in Depānama and unlikely to fall out of favor anytime soon. What of our aloof hero, the buffalo herdsman? The new emerging workforce of Depānama required familiarity with industrialization and mechanization and had neither time nor patience to spare. He, with his relaxed laidback style, would find it difficult fitting in with the new crew.

19

Night Out for the Village

When the television came to Depānama, it had to find its place in a routine where the radio was already well established. As soon as we awoke on weekday mornings, my mother switched on the radio. The sound of traditional drumbeats and the blowing of conch shell horns were a signature tune and prelude to the morning news by the Broadcasting Corporation. It started the frenzy that was the weekday morning in our home. No other sound gave us cause for so much activity. The urgent emotionless tones of the newscasters prodded us through our usual breakfast of bread and butter, with fruit jam or lentil curry. We listened listlessly to reports of the outcome of parliamentary sessions, budget crises, and debt resolution while we awaited our turn to use the only bathroom in the house. When the news drew to an end and the voices of the announcers became more relaxed, we knew it was time to make a final check of our school bags. My parents, my brother, and I piled into our car for the trip to Colombo, for work and school, at the very second the newscast ended, just before the daily programming schedule of songs, chats, interviews, and dramas began. The morning newscast was not only heard within our house, but it was also heard in all corners of the village, from our closest neighbors to the farthest ones.

The house to the left of ours belonged to Sirisena, the car mechanic. His petite wife, Karunawathie, listened to a small battery-operated radio as she went about her morning chores in the small mud kitchen behind their main house. The coconut leaf thatched roof was very low, just high enough to accommodate Karunawathie's height of about four feet or so. It allowed just room enough for her to sit by the fireplaces mounted on the floor. She did not have the luxury of having a cook or a maid and awoke while still dark, well before dawn, to make not only the breakfast for her husband and four children, but also to make their lunch and get the preliminary preparations going for dinner. This was too early even for the news. At this time, before the news came on, various religious authorities gave short sermons of encouragement suitable for the start of the day. The radio kept Karunawathie company as she labored in her tiny space, while her husband and children caught an extra hour of sleep.

Further up, right along Borella-Kottāwa Road, Grandpa and Grandma Martin's house resonated with the monotones of the news-casters in the morning, followed by radio programs all through the day. The sound of their radio could be heard by anyone travelling on foot along the Borella-Kottāwa Road.

Behind our house, in the house of Sheila and her husband Wilson, the radio was played particularly loudly since the return of their son from overseas. While abroad, he had acquired a taste for English pop songs. When he came back home to Depānama, he brought with him a radio with a cassette player on which he played his favorite songs, one after the other. Their property opened onto the Avenue of the Brave and the selections on their radio left no doubt in anyone passing their home that a recent overseas traveler had returned to the village.

Our family was by no means lacking in our own radio star. This honor belonged to the elder daughter of my Middle Aunt who was invited to sing in the popular children's program *The Uncle on the Moon.* My brother and I listened to this half-hour program each weekday afternoon on our radio at home. It featured songs sung by children and children's stories recited by hosts and special guests. After weeks of anticipation and constant reminders by my Middle Aunt not to miss the date and time, my brother and I sat as close as possible to the wooden box speakers of our radio to listen to the song our cousin had practiced. The program was broadcast live. The hostess was in the habit of asking a few questions from each child before the recitation and, in my cousin's case, the questions and appropriate answers had been rehearsed many times. Even before she answered, we knew what she would say. But this cousin was not a child of predictable habits and, as we listened to her soft voice coming through the speakers, both my brother and I could not avoid a sense of apprehension that our long association with her had instilled in us. The hostess asked my cousin what she did in her leisure. "Draw," she replied clearly, as we expected she would. "And child, what do you draw?" she inquired next. "Flowers and houses," my cousin replied without hesitation. If the hostess had known our cousin as well as we did, she would have then stopped and asked her to sing her song. But the hostess pressed further. "What else?" she asked. My cousin thought for a moment. "Toilets!" she replied definitively. My cousin did get her chance to sing after this, but we soon forgot what she sang. Her lapse in etiquette, however, was remembered for a long time afterwards.

Āchchā's home was not as quiet as was ours during the day. My younger cousins, the children of my Youngest Aunt, were home most of the day and my Youngest Aunt did not work, as did my mother and Middle Aunt. She and Āchchā listened to their respective radio programs from opposite sides of the living room on their respective radios. Āchchā's radio was a red pocket radio given to her by my father. "This is just what I wanted," she said when my father presented it to her. She kept it on her pillow and listened to religious sermons at dawn and at dusk. She kept it on her lap and listened to instructions when she practiced meditation. She carried it in her handbag to the temple and listened to talks and discourses while sitting under the *bo-fig* tree. On the full moon day, if she couldn't go to the temple to observe the Precepts of Discipline, she listened to them on the radio and observed the Precepts at home.

Āchchā's radio was heard only in her room, the third room on the right. It was not heard in the living room, the hallway, or the kitchen, but my Youngest Aunt's radio was. She listened to programs on cooking, health, and fashion in the afternoon. She liked to listen to sad love songs by popular artists all day until the evening newscast, when the beating of drums and the blowing of conch shell horns on the radio brought an end to her day.

Even before a television station was built, my Uncle Dhaham had had the foresight to purchase a television when returning from living abroad. Because the new transmission station was being built at the time but was not yet complete, they left the television in the big cardboard box it came in. The day the first transmission began was widely publicized both in the newspapers and on the radio. Ahead of time, my Uncle Dhaham bought an antenna and affixed it to the roof. He set the television on a small side table in the corner of the living room. My Youngest Aunt arranged a couch, my grandfather's long reclining chair, and several stools around the television. The television became the central point of interest in Āchchā's living room from the very first moment it was plugged in. At first, all the programs telecasted were foreign imports. In this, the radio was at a clear advantage. All of the programs broadcast over the radio were produced locally with local flare and flavor. Some programs running for years had achieved iconic status.

The radio hosts were well known and the voices of well-known people could frequently be heard over the radio.

In homes across the village, just as at Āchchā's place, radios played unobtrusively through the day as the householders went about their daily chores. The television, however, demanded time, attention, and a break from the daily routine. In those days, time dedicated to doing nothing was a precious commodity. The cost of a television was also prohibitive. The overall feeling in the village in these early times was that television was nothing more than a temporary distraction, and an expensive one at that.

The entire width and breadth of the living room at Āchchā's place had always been visible to the road when the wide veranda doors were open, and never more so than when the television was placed in it. No matter where in the living room the small fourteen-inch television was placed, there would be passersby along the Borella-Kottāwa Road who stopped in front of the Elephant Gates for a peek at it, whether it was on or off. Transmissions only began after dark and lasted only about three hours each day, but this practice of peering at the television from the roadside occurred from the time the veranda doors were opened in the morning to the time they were closed, when the household retired for bed.

After our evening meal, my parents, brother, and I often made the trip to Āchchā's place to watch television. The evening transmission started off with the American-produced *Sesame Street* program for children. In it, animals were humanized in the form of puppets and cartoons and attributed human characteristics and emotions. This was a novel and interesting concept for my young cousins. My parents, aunts, and uncles discussed the differences in the way in which words were pronounced on either side of the Atlantic. As children, they had attended school during the colonial occupation and had deep-rooted opinions about language acquired during this time.

Āchchā's living room had never been brightly lit, and in the evenings the flickering light of the television shone out through the Elephant Gates like a beacon. All who passed by and all who had heard of the television were drawn to it like moths to a flame. When so many had gathered at the Elephant Gates that their presence was impossible to ignore, my Uncle Dhaham would call out a greeting and invite the villagers in. The veranda would slowly fill with people craning for a glimpse of the television.

As the television station acquired more experience, programs of local production began to be transmitted on a regular basis and their schedules published weekly in the newspapers. It was then that the spectators at Āchchā's place began to get more organized and people came to sit on the veranda steps to see programs of their choice, and not just for a glimpse the box of light itself.

Saturday night was film night at Āchchā's place. A film, popular from the local cinema, would be telecast over the television on Saturday nights. Its name would be published in the national newspaper. Whether the newspaper was read or not by the time Friday evening rolled around, everyone in Depānama knew the name of the film, the actors, actresses, and plot that was showing Saturday night at Āchchā's place. If Āchchā was seen in her usual spot in the armchair, women passing by the Elephant Gates couldn't resist calling out and inquiring if "film night" was on. "I know nothing of these things," Āchchā would reply if she cared to reply at all. Even though Āchchā rarely professed any interest in matters pertaining to the television, my grandfather's long reclining chair was placed for her with a good view of the screen. When Āchchā retired to her room, my Uncle Dhaham usually occupied this place of prominence.

The Deer Hamlet was a long-running and popular radio drama. Its beloved characters had become household names. *The Deer Hamlet* was made into a black-and-white film. With this, a dream of loyal fans, many of whom had followed the radio drama for years and fantasized about what the characters looked like, was realized. It was shown in theaters to sold-out audiences for many months, several years prior to the arrival of the television.

Its story was set in a secluded hamlet in the middle of a tropical jungle. Its hero was named Kadira, a rugged character who was a little rough around the edges. His only attire was a loincloth. He battled savage beasts and poisonous snakes on a daily basis. As with every hero, there was a lady who had captured his heart, but hesitated before giving her heart to him. If this story line weren't captivating enough by itself, a whole host of bandits and vagabonds disrupted the tranquility of this quiet hamlet and plotted against Kadira. However challenging Kadira found the circumstances of his life to be, he never faltered in his righteous principles. The chief administrator and dignitary of the hamlet was an ineffective personality. He, together with his wife, provided the comic relief of the story line.

On the day of the telecast of *The Deer Hamlet*, people started to arrive at Āchchā's place well ahead of time to secure a place with a good view of the television screen. Save for emptying the veranda of the armchairs and opening the veranda doors as wide as possible, there was no other allowance that could be made for the crowds that gathered. My Youngest Aunt laid out mats on the floor, which was the only seating that could be provided for so many under the circumstances. A sea of people sat all around the living room floor that night and overflowed onto the steps of the veranda. At the start of the film, my Uncle Dhaham switched off the living room lights. There was no need to call for silence. Not even a whisper was heard. The television was slowly, but surely, finding its place.

20

The Third Room on the Right

When my Youngest Aunt married my Uncle Dhaham, Āchchā relinquished the responsibility of the running of the house to the new couple. The third bedroom on the right side of the house held a table for her books, an *almirah*—a tall wooden cupboard with several compartments and drawers—for her clothes, and a bed. This was all that was now hers.

Āchchā was my first friend and soul mate. She must have held me in her arms the very day I arrived, but if she recollected this day, she never discussed it with me. I have no memory of the first day I became aware of her presence in my life, but we became friends very fast, as granddaughters are likely to do with their grandmothers. This is especially so if they are the firstborn of many grandchildren and the favorite, as I believed myself to be. I called her Āchchā. It did not occur to me as a youngster that she had any other name than the one I had given her. It seemed to suit her naturally. Much later I learned her name was Grace.

Āchchā slept in a four-poster bed. No nightstands or nightlights flanked its sides. She did not use a footstool or a floor mat, and so the bed stood alone in the center of her room. The headboard had a design of radiating rays, which met in the middle, carved into the wood. Each ray had two sloping sides, like those of a mountain. It was not an ornate bed, but rather one with geometric shapes of circles and lines. At each corner of the bed was a stump that stood about three feet off the mattress with empty cylindrical metal brackets where its posts would have been fitted. I can never remember seeing posts fitted on the stumps. My brother and I would climb onto the bed and hide pens, erasers, marbles, and pebbles in these cylindrical brackets. Whatever we kept in Āchchā's room was safe until we returned to reclaim it. She didn't mind that we kept our drawings, essays, pictures, and books on her table, safe from the prying hands of my young cousins. She kept my sewing box containing the sewing projects we did together on top of her *almirah*.

Āchchā slept on a coir mattress, which was probably the harshest material that a mattress could possibly be made from. The ends of the coir sometimes poked through the sheets and were prickly to the touch. I tried to solve this problem by pulling at the ends of the coir, but this only made it worse, for the coir stuck out even more and never came out completely. At the head end, two pillows were placed side by side. They were neither plump nor soft, and even when placed one atop the other, gave only the slightest elevation to the head. Āchchā had no electric fan like we did in our room at home. A series of circular openings high on the wall provided ventilation from the outside, but it also let mosquitoes in. To me, her room and accommodations lacked some basic comforts and I wondered how comfortable Āchchā was at night. "Unnecessary comforts promote aches and pains," she explained. "I sleep very well in this room," she reassured me. The sheets were coarse white cotton with pale pastel stripes running lengthwise. The foot end of the bed always had a little sand on it from Āchchā's barefooted walks in the garden and the house. My younger cousins who lived at Āchchā's place would leave behind an occasional spot or streak of dust. They liked to run in from the garden and jump on Āchchā's bed. Āchchā had hung a framed photograph of her husband across from the head end of her bed, and though she never mentioned it in so many words, I knew it must have been that she needed to see his image upon waking up and welcoming a new day.

When my brother and I had knelt under Āchchā's bed, when we were looking for stray pencils or marbles, a faint rancid odor greeted us. The source of the odor was Āchchā's "night pot," a tin pot with a wide mouth and two handles on either side. At first its discovery had filled us with curiosity, but when I saw the rust stains on the blue and white mottled enamel I had guessed what she needed it for. The only bathroom at Kshānti led off the hallway in the back next to the kitchen. At night, if Āchchā needed to get to it, she would have had to open the wide double doors leading out of the living room to the back of the house and make her way along the hallway in darkness. She would have used the night pot in her room instead.

When my parents went out to parties and dinners in Colombo, we got dropped off at Āchchā's place. On these nights, we slept on Āchchā's bed. I was careful to dust away the sand at the foot of the bed before we got in and slap at any mosquitoes before switching off the light. My Youngest Aunt would temporarily place a pedestal fan for us in Āchchā's room. Yet, despite its breeze, it was difficult to fall asleep. The muffled noise of the television in the living room, the whirring of the mosquitoes, and the sudden mechanical buzz of a passing motorist kept sleep at bay until Āchchā came to bed. She had a spot between my brother and me, for we both wanted to be next to her. I would reach for her hands and feel her bony arms with the delicate wrinkled skin wrap around me before eventually drifting off to sleep.

Āchchā's *almirah* stood in a corner of her room. It matched her bed. She kept a few saris, jackets, housecoats, and undergarments in it. She also kept the few items of jewelry and the deeds to her properties locked in her *almirah*. The keys to the *almirah* and the keys to the house she kept in a large bunch, usually on her table.

In the corner of her room, opposite her *almirah*, was Āchchā's table. It was a simple wooden table without drawers or attached cupboards. Those items she did not keep in her *almirah*, she kept on her table. She had a collection of religious books. These were old editions of even older books with texts impossible to read, much less grasp the meaning of. She also kept several stacks of notebooks on her table because she liked to keep things written down. I suppose it was a habit she had acquired as a schoolteacher. When Āchchā had transferred to the school at Polwatte, things had become easier, my Youngest Aunt told me. The commute to work was so short she could walk. She did not have to take the bus as she did to the school at Maharagama.

Āchchā's notebooks were yellow with age, their pages worn thin with frequent turning. The strong smell of glue and wood that new books gave off had long since dissipated, leaving a faint odor of ink and dust. My Youngest Aunt had taught me how to wrap my books in brown paper covers. If Āchchā ever covered her books, the brown paper covers too were worn, their corners falling away, macerated with use.

In Āchchā's books she wrote religious verses and stanzas with explanations and translations. She didn't keep a daily diary, but kept records of her travels on pilgrimages. When she wrote accounts and expenses, the numbers she wrote had not the mechanical quality that numbers expressing technicalities always had, but they too told a story. I looked into Āchchā's books and discovered that it was not just on sweet treats and presents for her grandchildren that she spent her money. She also paid the laundry lady, the coconut plucker, the specialty cooks that came for the New Year, and the seamstress who made her white lace jackets. These accounts were settled and carefully recorded by her.

I learned to read and write my first letters from Āchchā. I tried hard to achieve the same antiquated flowing quality of her penmanship. My brother preferred playing with my cousins to sitting down with Āchchā. He was also younger than me. "He has not learnt to write from Āchchā and now his writing will be as bad as mine," joked my father.

Though it seemed that we were always at Āchchā's, she visited us frequently in our home too. In the afternoons when the heat and humidity of midday had begun to ease, if Āchchā had nothing else to do, she came over to visit us in our home. She dressed in an Indian sari as she usually did for casual outings, tucked her purse under her arm, and set off with her umbrella held up against the setting sun. At this time, the branches of our jack trees cast a patchwork of long shadows on our winding gravel driveway. When Āchchā, having entered through our gates, strolled leisurely down it, it was as if the shadows themselves moved. As a child, I sat on the couch in our living room and watched for the moving shadows in our driveway, hoping to be surprised by the emergence of Āchchā's figure from within the moving shadows.

It was I, more than my brother, who enjoyed these visits from Āchchā. We were away from the constant proximity of my Youngest Aunt and free to chat and gossip in confidence about matters that were confidential to the two of us. We started off these intimate afternoons with a cup of tea. To accompany her tea, I made for her the only recipe I knew how to make in those days: two pieces of buttered toast sprinkled with sugar. She accepted these refreshments with a smile. She assured me that my sugared toast was the most delectable snack she had ever had.

When Āchchā's last grandchild, the second daughter of my Middle Aunt, was born, Āchchā came over to our home more frequently. My Middle Aunt lived closer to our home than to hers, and when Āchchā came over to our home, my Middle Aunt's daughter was brought over to ours. She was a sweet, happy, and gentle toddler with a round face and a mass of bouncy curls. Her disposition was a direct and relieving contrast to the rough and tumble habits of Āchchā's two grandsons, the sons of my Youngest Aunt, whose company she endured all day. The games we played with this cousin were tame compared to the games we played with the boys. We liked to make her run, just to watch her curls spring up and down. Āchchā watched us sitting on the garden bench on our lawn.

When Āchchā first got heart pains, she was admitted to the nursing home at Nugegoda. I had never seen her sick before and had never known her to complain. My brother and I were taken to see her in her hospital room. This was so different from the familiar third room on the right at Kshānti we were used to seeing her in. "Did I scare you?" she asked, holding my hand. I smiled down at her as she lay in the strange bed on cold starched white sheets. I was puzzled by her question. I did not know there was anything to fear, because Āchchā had always been very robust. She returned home, but soon after had more heart pains. When my parents, aunts, and uncles left in the night to take her to the hospital in Colombo, we felt vaguely uneasy. Āchchā did not return home again to Kshānti to the third room on the right. In the afternoons I watched our driveway, wanting to see the shadows move and her familiar figure emerge. The shadows moved, but it was only the wind.

Author Q&A

What motivated you to write a memoir about your birthplace?

For me, this book is a bridge to my place of origin. One day when my memory fails me, the bridge I have built through the words I have written will still be standing. My own words will transport and comfort me. It is the miracle of the written word that it transcends time, without aging or fading, and never more so than in the age we live in now. It is my hope that my readers will be inspired to build their own bridges with their own words and create for themselves a source of solace that transcends time.

Were you inspired by a similar story?

As a young teenager, I read a series of stories published in the *Daily News*—a leading newspaper in Sri Lanka. These were chapters from a book called *Grass for My Feet* by J. Vijayatunga, first published in London in 1935. The author was a Sri Lankan like me, who had migrated to Great Britain. I was so enchanted by these magical stories that I cut them out of the paper and pasted them in my scrapbook. I brought these scrapbook stories with me to the United States when I migrated. Through the resources available on the Internet, I was able to track down a single volume in a small family-owned bookstore in Denver, Colorado. It took the proprietress of the store about two days to find it among their inventory. To this day, this volume is one of my most treasured possessions. It was autographed by the author in 1947.

Your family uses proper names, birth order, and pet names when addressing relatives. Is this a cultural convention?

Using the birth order to address a close relative is a mark of affection, such as in the case of my Youngest and Middle Aunts. Pet names like Milk Uncle and Little Mamma are used to address close relatives. The use of the proper name indicates some distance in the bloodline. I do not use birth order when addressing any of my uncles, who are related to me only by marriage, but use their proper names with the prefix "Uncle." There was more than one coconut plucker, cook of sweet meats, tree trimmer, and buffalo herdsman in the village, but I did not know each of them individually by name. Then there were those in the village who were one of a kind, like the Bucket, the Belly, and Peethara. By any other name, they would have been just as memorable.

In your portrayal of Āchchā, it appears that she has endeared herself to you all over again as an adult. What about her is endearing to you now?

Preformed judgments, preconceived notions, and prejudice played a large part in the social structure and function of the village. I am sure Āchchā had her prejudices and preconceived notions about the village, but she kept them to herself. She did not impose her standards upon me. I was free to form my own opinions. After all, is that not what every child wants? The freedom to form opinions based upon his or her own judgment? In her presence, I was free.

How did Āchchā adapt to the transition from being the lady of the house to being a guest in her own home?

Tradition dictated that the ancestral house pass on to the youngest child, whether male or female, upon marriage. If the youngest child is female, the ancestral house is offered as part of her dowry. Just as the rice fields succumbed to submersion by the monsoon rains, Āchchā's generation succumbed to tradition as being natural law. Tradition was neither to be questioned nor resisted. Āchchā had prepared for this eventuality from the time she conceived her first child. Her needs at the time she made the transition were few, easily accommodated within the confines of the third room on the right. She adapted to change in the only way she knew how—with grace.

As a child you, just as much as Āchchā in her retirement, observed the village through the Elephant Gates rather than become part of its fabric. Why was this?

When my brother and I were born, my mother started us on a journey to distance ourselves from the village, from a place she saw as being backward and unprogressive. She strived tirelessly and single-mindedly on behalf of our education as a way out of this stupor. Her mission eventually became my mission too, and our aspirations became as one. Āchchā observed the village through the Elephant Gates because her life's chores were already done. I did not venture beyond the Elephant Gates because my life's chores had not yet begun.

It seems that Āchchā's death signaled the ultimate change—how did life change after her death?

For some years my mother assumed the matriarchal role of our extended family. My mother, however, was not the unbiased authority that Āchchā was. My mother had the final word on many things, but not everything. Instead of meeting up at Kshānti on New Year's Day, my extended family met at our home. Among other things, playing cricket with my cousins and uncles on our lawn on New Year's Day became a new tradition for us. There was a time when disputes arose between my mother and her sisters about the division of the rice fields, and Āchchā's daughters feuded. Eventually time healed these wounds. Today they have reinforced the bonds they formed as children at Kshānti more than half a century ago.

The name of Kshānti itself fell out of favor and a number was assigned to the ancestral house, as was required by the postal service. The Elephant Gates and the gate posts were removed and the entrance moved to the side of the house when the Borella-Kottāwa Road was broadened. The house itself was renovated. A pair of new gates was installed. Despite these changes, my Youngest Aunt has kept her doors, the doors of what used to be Kshānti, open with a warm message of welcome to all her nieces and nephews, now with families of their own.

In subtle ways you indicate that your father had a need to belong to the village. Why?

My father wanted a place to belong after uprooting himself from his hometown. He was far more indulgent when it came to the village and the villagers than was my mother. He was indulgent because he saw things from an outsider's perspective, which sometimes provides a clearer view. He saw the simplicity of village life not as a choice but as a compulsion born of poverty and hardship. He found employment in Colombo for village youth whenever he could. He was generous when he paid village tradesmen. When our coconut palms and jack trees got raided in the night, he did not get upset. He could not resist an opportunity to get involved. His naiveté, however, meant that his empathy was sometimes misplaced, his efforts not always successful, and his need for validation often misunderstood.

When in 2005 he passed away from cancer, he made his final journey down Cemetery Road to the cemetery of Depānama. In death he became what in life he could not—a true villager. This is why this book is dedicated to *Thāththi*, which means "father."

Is there a layer of symbolism other than the finality of death behind your description of the village funeral procession down Cemetery Road?

The final journey down Cemetery Road is symbolic of unity in death, regardless of station in life, when inequality is finally equalized. In the village, inequality was commonplace and pervaded every aspect of daily life. For some visiting Kshānti to enter through the front door and for others to enter through the back door was expected etiquette. For some to sit on high chairs, for some to sit on low chairs, and still for others to sit on the front step was not seen as inequality but as decorum. Death is the great equalizer of humanity.

Do you regret the dispersion of your extended family and the loss of the traditions you practiced within it?

The definition of family is wide and varied. It is not just bonds of blood and common origin that bring people together in modern times. Friendship, common goals, and shared struggles bring people together as families. Some of these bonds are fleeting and others last a lifetime, but bonds so made always leave a lasting impression. Traditions need not necessarily be time-honored rituals but practices within our daily situations that make our lives more meaningful. The diversity of the family of the current age and the creation of new traditions are reasons to rejoice.

About the Author

Chamalee Weeratunge is a practicing physician, specializing in Infectious Disease. She lives in Austin, Texas, with her husband and son, having moved to the US from Sri Lanka in 1999 for a residency in Internal Medicine in Brooklyn, New York. Prior to living in Austin she was an Infectious Disease fellow in San Antonio, where she met her husband. This is her first book.

Made in the USA
San Bernardino, CA
17 February 2016